Nathan Jves
The author is the founder and the Secretary-General of the Action Committee on American-Arab Relations. He received his high school diploma at the Baghdad School of Commerce, and obtained his B.A., M.A., and Ph.D. in political science at the University of California.

Dr. Mehdi has written many articles, pamphlets, and books. His books include a comparative study entitled CONSTITUTIONALISM: WESTERN AND MIDDLE EASTERN. In A NATION OF LIONS . . . CHAINED, he took issue with William Lederer, who had described America as A NATION OF SHEEP. Dr. Mehdi received the Book of the Year Award of the Association of the Friends of Literature in Beirut, Lebanon for his A NATION OF LIONS . . . CHAINED.

Author and lecturer, Dr. Mehdi has addressed many college and university audiences and civic clubs throughout the United States, and has appeared on the several radio and television networks. His academic interest is in the fields of jurisprudence and constitutional law, and logical empiricism.

In the interest of peace in the Middle East, Dr. Mehdi proposed on 25 March 1966 to go to Israel and discuss with Israeli leaders and people the question of peace in that region. His was the first proposal of its kind. In November and December of 1966, he visited the Arab world, meeting with Arab kings and heads of state in the interest of peace, and better American-Arab relations.

Peace

In

The

Middle East

M. T. MEHDI

Table of Contents

Dedication
TO THE YOUNG LIBERALS
AND INTELLECTUALS
OF THE WORLD.

Preface

In 1896, Theodore Herzl of Austria wrote his pamphlet, THE JEWISH STATE, calling for the establishment of a Jewish state in Palestine.

In 1917, Britain, not the Arab people of Palestine, issued the Balfour Declaration, viewing with favor the establishment of a Jewish national home in Palestine with a contradictory *proviso* supposedly to protect Arab rights.

When the Balfour Declaration was issued in 1917, the population of Palestine was 93% Moslem and Christian and 7% Jewish. In 1922, the total population of Palestine was 752,048: the Jews numbered 83,790; the Christians and Moslems 660,441; with 7,617 others.

In 1922, the League of Nations, not the Palestine Arabs, assigned to Britain a Mandate over Palestine in order to fulfill the terms of the British Balfour Declaration.

In 1947, the United Nations, not the Arabs of Palestine, partitioned Palestine and led to the creation of the Jewish State of Israel and the displacement of the Palestine Arab people.

Of course, the Arab people of Palestine did not consent to any of these declarations and promises to the Jews, nor did they consent to the partition of Palestine. On the contrary, they objected, opposed and fought against each step from the Balfour Declaration to the Partition Plan and the establishment of the Jewish State.

While it is understandable that the Arabs should oppose foreign, Jewish or otherwise, intrusion into their homes, there are many people in the western countries who seem to be unable to understand the Arab position and objection. Indeed, many persons of good intention had expressed the thought that the Arabs would be happy and pleased with the arrival of the Jews in Palestine and the establishment of the Jewish state. Many felt that the new Jewish state would be a source of progress and peace in the interest of the Arabs. Many who expressed astonishment at Arab opposition felt that sooner or later the Arabs would come to accept the new state and would be benefited by the blessings of the new progressive western style "democracy" in the Middle East. In his memoirs, President Harry S. Truman expressed the hope, albeit naively, and from the Arab viewpoint, insulting, that Israel would become the industrial center to which Arab raw material would be brought and from which Israeli manufactured goods would be sent to Arab markets.

Today, after some nineteen years, it is evident that the Arabs are as adamant and as opposed to foreign Jewish intrusion as ever, and are determined as ever to regain their homes. Invariably, every year the Director of the United Nations Relief and Work Agency (UNRWA) has been reporting to the General Assembly that the Arab refugees have the most intense emotional desire and determination to go back home.

More recently, the Arabs of Palestine have been able to organize themselves in the Palestine Liberation Organization (PLO), which even if today is more of a paper organization, it will eventually develop into a full-fledged governmental apparatus with a well-trained army, regular as well as guerrilla, to regain the lost homeland. The activities of "al-fateh," the small but effective Palestine guerrilla commando force, disclosed first in January 1964, represent only the beginning of a long struggle by Palestinian Arabs to regain their homes from the foreign intruders.

It is abundantly clear now, in 1967, that the prospects of peace in the Middle East are nil, and the possibilities of war loom vividly on the horizon.

We wish to prevent the advent of war in the Middle East, and bring about a peaceful solution to the conflict in that region. Hence, this book, which is addressed to men of good will everywhere, including Jews, Christians and Moslems. It is an appeal to all who are concerned with peace and the actual good of the human individuals who are involved in the dilemma of an imminent war — a war which would engulf the human race unless efforts toward its prevention are made by all concerned.

This book is the reply to Herzl's quest. The ultimate goal of Herzl was to eliminate the "Jewish question." His JEW-ISH STATE was the vehicle for the attainment of that goal.

Today, however, the Jewish state has been in existence for nearly two decades, but the Jewish question has not been resolved. Herzl and other early Zionists had thought that after the establishment of the Jewish state, the Jews of the *Diaspora* would go *en masse* to the Jewish state, and the few who might not wish to go there would be assimilated in the societies of which they were a part, and thus, there would be no longer any "Jewish question."

At present, however, the majority of world Jews have refused to go to Israel, and hence, the Herzlian expectations and quest have not been fulfilled.

In presenting what may be the only possible peaceful solution to the conflict in the Middle East, I wish also to provide a satisfactory answer to Herzl's hope to resolve the Jewish question.

When Herzl wrote THE JEWISH STATE in 1896, he sowed the seeds of conflict and war in the Middle East. My interest is peace, and hence, the title of this book, PEACE IN THE MIDDLE EAST.

New York City   M. T. Mehdi
15 May 1967

I

The Problem

To propose a solution to the conflict in the Middle East, it is of utmost importance to know the nature of the conflict, and to know the nature of the conflict, one has to know about the arguments of the parties to the conflict. Hence, this chapter will present broad outlines of some of the major claims and counter-claims of the parties to the dispute over Palestine.

The question of Palestine, which may lead to a third world war, is basically the result of the immigration of Jews, mostly Europeans, into Palestine — which had been inhabited by the Arabs for centuries — against the will of the Arabs, but with British, and later American, and general western support. It must be made clear that the conflict is not between the Arabs and the Jews, as commonly considered; it is a conflict between the Arabs and other non-Zionists on the one hand, and the Zionist Jews and their supporters on the other.

Zionism is a political movement which claims that Palestine belongs to the Jews. The Zionist movement has based its claim on "historical grounds," and has appealed to religious and humanitarian sentiments. In the process of achieving its goal, it has applied political and economic pressure, as well as many other techniques.

The major Zionist argument is advanced in terms of a special theory of historical "right." It maintains that Palestine belongs to the Jews because some two thousand years ago, certain Jews used to live in Palestine. And as the Jews, according to Zionism, have lived in exile during the last two thousand years, they are entitled, as a matter of historical "right," to go "back home."

The second supporting argument is offered in the name of the Bible to the effect that God had promised Palestine to the Jews, and the Jewish return to Palestine is in fulfillment of a Biblical prophesy.

The third supporting argument advanced by the Zionists is that the Jews were persecuted and mistreated in Europe, and thus were in desperate need of a place of their own. Palestine was such a place.

A fourth argument advanced is that the Jews have improved the land in Palestine better than the Arabs, with the implication that because of this "Jewish know-how," the Jews are entitled to the land. Of course, in order to ascribe legitimacy to this position, the Zionists refer continuously to Arab backwardness and the Jewish achievements and progress, and to the fact that the Jews can teach the Arabs and can raise the standard of living in the Middle East.

There are many other arguments advanced by the Zionists regarding the details of the problem. These include questions of land ownership in Palestine; the claim that Arab feudalists and corrupt governments oppose Israel; that the United Nations had given Palestine to the Jews; that in 1948, the Arabs had attacked the Jews; that the Arab people of Palestine left Palestine voluntarily and of their own accord due to the instigation of the Arab leaders; and that the Arab leaders do not wish to resettle the Arab refugees in order to use them as political pawns. There are also claims that Israel is a bastion of democracy, that it is the miracle of the twentieth century, and so on and so forth.

I have analysed these claims in my book, A NATION OF LIONS . . . CHAINED.[1] I believe it is in order to record here the various positions regarding some of the major points and arguments. And the major points revolve around the questions of "historical right," which is the theoretical rationale for Zionism; and the question of European persecution of the Jews, which is the actual factor that led to the full manifestation of Zionism and the "achievement" of its goal.

1. On Historical Right

The major Zionist premise that Palestine belongs to the Jews because some two thousand years ago certain Jews used to live there, is an illogical claim and an argument which is naturally unacceptable to the Arabs as it would be unacceptable to any other people. Should such an historical claim be admitted, then the whole map of the world would have to be changed. Everyone would have the "right" to go to any country with which he could claim an historical tie. In the era of modern nationalism, such claims could not stand. Otherwise, many a Russian citizen may have a claim to Alaska, and many a Mexican would be entitled to California. Furthermore, the Arabs, on their part, would have claims and rights to Spain, which used to belong to the Arabs; and the American Indians would have the right to Manhattan as well as the rest of the American continent.

Indeed, there is no basis in law or logic which would vest any group of people today with rights to other lands on the ground that some people of the claimant's religion or race had conquered that land and occupied it many many centuries ago.

The Arabs will not accept, and cannot be expected to accept, any concept of "historical right" of European Jews to Palestine. For David Ben-Gurion and Levy Eshkol are Europeans as much as Arthur J. Goldberg and Jacob K. Javits are Americans.

It is indeed in the interest of the Jews themselves that this position should be rejected and refuted at the outset. To say that the home of Ambassador Arthur J. Goldberg, who represents the United States of America at the United Nations, is Palestine and/or Israel, is indeed ridiculous. Ambassador Arthur J. Goldberg's home is no place whatever other than the United States of America. If we admit that his home is Palestine and/or Israel, just because he is a Jew, then he surely has no business being the representative of the United States at the United Nations.

The Zionist position is indeed dangerous, not only to the Arabs whose home they have invaded and taken over, but also to the majority of the Jews of the world, who are members and citizens of their respective countries.

Of course, when Herzl and other early Zionists wrote about the Jewish state, they contemplated an end to the so-called "Jewish question." Their thinking was that the Jews from the various countries would go to Palestine, and that those Jews who refuse to "go back" will gradually become assimilated in the countries in which they reside, and thus the "Jewish question" would be resolved. However, it is evident that that solution has not come about as a result of the creation of Israel, or, indeed, despite the creation of Israel.

The Jews are members of the various societies and citizens

of the various countries and the claim and argument that they are "from" Israel or "belong" to Israel or have rights to Palestine are illogical as well as dangerous ones.

The Jews have no right, collective or otherwise, to Palestine, any more than American Catholics have a right to Rome. An American Irishman might love Ireland, and may have all the spiritual ties to St. Patrick's Day, when he might wear some green. But he has no "right" to go to Ireland if the people of Ireland do not permit him to go there and consent to his admission.

Indeed, a Moslem from America who might have a religious obligation to go to Mecca, has no legal right to go to Mecca without the specific permission of the people of Arabia. Likewise, a Moslem from Indonesia with a strong feeling of religious obligation to make the pilgrimage to Mecca, cannot go there, despite his spiritual ties to Mecca, if the people of Arabia do not permit him to go.

Hence, any Jewish intrusion into Palestine, notwithstanding any claim as to spiritual or historical ties to Palestine, would not grant the foreign Jews a right to go to Palestine without the permission of the people of Palestine. The Arab people of Palestine have not granted such permission to foreign Jews to go into Palestine.

Of course, on the question of spiritual ties, let it be remembered that Christians have equally strong spiritual ties to the Holy Land as the Jews and the Moslems. To give the Jews this special favorable treatment is a violation of the rights of the Christians and the Moslems to their own spiritual ties to Palestine.

The Zionists' claim to historical right would make the Jews

who are living in countries other than Palestine/Israel foreigners living in exile. That is to say, according to the logic of Zionism, the Jews in America, England, Brazil, Egypt, Indonesia, and the Soviet Union, are "Israelis residing in exile." The Zionist position would certainly raise the question of double loyalty of the Zionist Jews. This leads to resentment, creates prejudice, and stimulates anti-Semitism. Whether the Zionist Jews want anti-Semitism to be perpetuated or want the elimination of Anti-Semitism, will be discussed in a forthcoming chapter. At any rate, the dubious position of the Zionists, stemming from the so-called "historical claim," must be noted here, and it must be noted that the Arabs cannot accept such claims any more than any other people would accept a like assertion.

2. On Biblical Prophesies

Even though many of the Zionists are atheists and have no belief in prophesies, Biblical or otherwise, they advance and use nevertheless a Biblical argument as a vehicle to support their claim and position. They maintain that the Bible has promised them and offered them the right to Palestine.

However, Biblical scholars have pointed out that Genesis 12:7, "Unto thy seed will I give this land," and other Biblical quotations referring to the children of Abraham, include the Arabs, both Moslem and Christian, even perhaps before these Biblical references might include Messrs. David Ben-Gurion and Abba Eban. The fact is that the Arab Moslems and Christians are descendants of the children of Abraham; whereas the majority of the European Jews are of Slavic or Polish ancestry. Accordingly, and if one believes in prophesies, the Biblical prophesy was fulfilled when Palestine was reverted to these Arab "seeds of Abraham," and became an Arab land. Indeed, many of the Palestinian Arabs might be the descendants of the people who had lived in Palestine long before the Jews had ever gone to Palestine. It is possible that some amongst them might be the direct descendants of the Jews of Palestine, who later accepted Christianity, and some of whom later converted to Islam. At any rate, the ties of the people of Palestine to Palestine and their title to that land go back some 5,000 years, if the Jewish claims go back 4,000 years.

Of course, it would be unreasonable to suppose that the Bible would support the proposition that the European Jews have a right to go to the home of the Christian and Moslem Arabs against their will. Nor do the rules of rational analysis support the Zionist claim. For it is not unreasonable to assume that the Arabs of Palestine are more entitled to their home than Mr. Ben-Gurion, a Pole, whose ancestors, along with other Slavic tribesmen, might have been converted to Judaism several hundred years ago. One wonders whether Palestine is also the home of the ancestors of Elizabeth Taylor, who was recently converted to Judaism, or the home of the ancestors of Sammy Davis, Jr.

But even if we assume that Mr. Ben-Gurion and other Jews were direct descendants of Abraham, still this does not entitle them to go to the home of the Arab "cousin" without the permission of the cousin: Just as Americans cannot go to England and Europe on the basis of an historical tie and European ancestry without British and/or European permission and consent.

Furthermore, the assertion that "the return of the Jews to Palestine is a fulfillment of Biblical prophesy and is based on historical right" cannot be supported by facts. The fact is that the Jews have *not* gone to Palestine. Of the total population of world Jewry, only 12% are now in Palestine/Israel, and 88% reside elsewhere. The fact is, then, that the Jews have not gone to Israel, and are not going to Israel, despite Zionism and its continued attempts to uproot the Jews from their various countries and take them to the new state.

There are some five and a half million Jews in America, and the doors, of course, are wide open for them to go to "their homeland," if they so desire. The anti-Semites, naturally, would like very much to ship these five and a half million American Jews and send them "home." To be sure, such an action would evoke the delight and approval of Levy Eshkol and Abba Eban and other inhumane and unprincipled Zionists. However, to say that at present the Jews have gone home, or are going home, is plainly absurd and without factual foundation except if we should advance the paradoxical position of stating that the minority of Jews who are in Israel constitute the majority, and the majority who have refused to go there constitute an insignificant minority.

It would seem that the majority of world Jews have repudiated Zionism, declined the "opportunity to go home," and prefer staying "in exile."[2]

Of course, even if we assume that on the basis of the Zionist Jewish conception of the Bible, the Jews can make certain claims of historical ties to Palestine, this claim would not impose any obligation upon the Christian and Moslem Arabs to accept the Jewish interpretation of the Bible. At any rate, the Palestinian Arabs, Christians and Moslems, have openly opposed and rejected such conception and/or misconception of the Bible. The Zionist Jewish conception that they had a right to Palestine is no more obligatory upon the Christian and Moslem Arabs than the messianic complex and belief of any group might impose any obligation upon any other group.

A distinguished Jewish scholar once defined Judaism in terms of Zionism: It is an integral part of the Jewish faith, and the Jewish religious obligation, that the Jews should go to Palestine/Israel. Accordingly, a Russian Jew has the religious obligation and therefore the right to go to the homes of the Christian and Moslem Palestinians.

Of course, the Jews may conceive of Judaism any way they wish, including a belief in a religious obligation to go to Palestine or anywhere else. But such a feeling of religious obligation would not entitle them to any right against other people.

If the Jewish religion does indeed obligate an American or any other Jew to go to the home of the Christian and Moslem Arabs, or to the home of anyone else, then the Jews should amend their religion and revise that element of their faith that obligates them to so trespass upon other people's rights. By the same token, if the Christians or Moslems believed that they had a religious obligation, and therefore a right, to intrude upon other lands, against the will of the people of those lands, then we would have to ask the Christians or Moslems to change and amend their religion, eliminating from it those parts which authorize or encourage trespassing upon the rights of others.

3. "Improvement of Land" and "Bastion of Democracy"

In their propaganda to support and justify their deed, the Zionist refer to the ability of the Jews to improve the land of Palestine, stress Arab backwardness, and describe Israel as a "bastion of democracy."

There are many issues involved here. Of course, the argument that the Jews can improve the land and therefore they have some legitimate ground to take over the land, is like the argument advanced by Adolf Hitler. Hitler, upon invading Poland, said that he was there to improve Polish agriculture, as the backward Poles were incapable of improving the land. This kind of argument is basically immoral and it is astounding that many a liberal who opposes the use of this argument by Hitler and the imperialists, would go on producing it on behalf of Zionist colonialism in Palestine.

The argument is also fallacious from a different viewpoint. The land was "improved" not because those who worked it were Moslems, Christians, or Jews, but because the people were westerners using modern western techniques and know-how. More specifically, the Jews were able to improve the land not because they were Jews, but because they were westerners. Oriental Jews have been incompetent and incapable of improving the land, and today they are the scum of the earth in Israel, discriminated against by the western Jews in a most shameful way. Then, of course, it is noteworthy to remember that some three billion dollars have been poured into Israel, and the Israelis had better improve the land with those three billion dollars.

In this connection, it is important to note that the little Arab state of Kuwait has achieved in the last ten or fifteen years in the various fields of economic, social and educational development what makes the entire Israeli "achievement" seem like a boy-scoutish endeavor. True, Kuwait was able to make this spectacular change because it has received money through the exploitation of its oil resources. By the same token, the Israelis have been able to improve as a result of the billions they received in terms of charity from abroad.

Furthermore, if a European Jew with a doctorate in soil chemistry goes to Palestine, or a Jewish graduate of the American Military Academy at West Point, such as David (Mickey) Marcus, goes there after renouncing his citizenship, he had better improve the agriculture or strengthen the Israeli army. To repeat, they can do these, not because they are Jews, but because they are products of western know-how.

Then we have to raise a basic question as to whether our concern is with the "land" or "the people who live on the land." If the Arab people of Palestine are deprived of their land and live in refugee camps, it would be facetious and wicked to go on talking about "improvement" of the land while the people of the land are impoverished and living in forced exile.

In this connection, one of the most astounding examples of the totalitarian nature of Zionist Jewish mentality is expressed in the form of the following argument and question: The territory the Jews occupy is so puny and the Arabs have large and gigantic lands; so why all the Arab objection to the little tiny piece of land which the Jews have occupied and are working so well?

I suggest that this is an example of the totalitarian nature of Zionist mentality because this argument disregards the individual, individual rights, and individual responsibility, and views the human person and his rights in some vague collective manner, irrelevant to the individual human person involved in the problem.

To demonstrate the situation: assume that some thieves and intruders steal the property of one Jacob Javits of New York, and destroy his home. Javits naturally would object, protest, and put up a big fight in an all out attempt to capture the thieves and recover the property. To argue that Javits should really not make so much of an issue because of the loss of his home and property on the ground that there are large property holdings in New York and that the Rockefeller estate, for instance, is a gigantic piece of land, and that Lyndon Baines Johnson has a huge ranch in Texas — to argue this way and thereby attempt to console Javits and make him seem ridiculous or at least unreasonable for his attempts to recover his property and home, such arguments are indeed either naively stupid or wickedly inhumane.

The fact that there is huge land and great wealth in New York, Texas, and elsewhere in America, is no substitute for the home and property of the individual Jacob Javits. Likewise, if the state of Alaska is invaded and occupied by the Russians on the ground that Alaska used to belong to the Russians, or on any other ground, and if the Americans put up a big fight, as they should, it would be ludicrous to console the Americans by suggesting that they should forget about Alaska on the ground that there are large unsettled pieces of land in other parts of the United States. The fact that there is much unsettled land in Arizona, New Mexico, Colorado, Texas, and so on, is no substitute in any way for an Alaska lost to the U.S.S.R.

Likewise, and by the same token, if there are lands in Iraq, Egypt, and in Arabia unoccupied, this is no substitute for the right of the Palestinians to their own land and homes in Palestine. The fact that Jacob Javits and Nelson Rockefeller are both New Yorkers does not mean that Javits should forget about his property which was lost, on the ground that Rockefeller is a rich landed gentry. By the same token, if there are some rich Arab kings and princes, this by no means pre-empts the right of the Palestinian Arabs to their land and property.

To argue that the people of Palestine should forget about their homes and land because some other Arabs are rich and possess unsettled land — to argue this way as the Zionists do, is stupid. But are the Zionists who continuously advance such arguments really stupid or do they think that other people are stupid enough to accept such fallacious arguments? Neither! I believe the reason for presenting such arguments lies in the totalitarian nature of the Zionist thinking and movement. Viewing the individual Jew as part of a collectivity even more than as an independent unit and entity unto himself, the Zionists conceive of the Arabs in the same collective way. But the Arabs, as other people, are individuals even before being parts of a collectivity. Let the Zionists recognize this fact. Furthermore, let the Zionists remember that other totalitarian movements, such as Nazism, were finally destroyed despite their power and initial success. Totalitarian thinking and movements have no place in the modern world!

*　*　*

Then there is the Zionist argument that Israel is a "bastion of democracy" in the midst of a sea of Arab dictatorships and backwardness. As a "Jewish state," Israel is a state which is based either on religion or on race. The concept of a "Jewish state," "Moslem state," or "Christian state" belongs to the sixteenth century and not to the twentieth century. A state based on race, such as the Aryan race of Nazi Germany, is likewise undemocratic.

It is astonishing that American politicians and many a liberal would go around talking about Israel as a democracy. The same liberals would object strongly if we say that "America is a Christian state" or that "America is a Caucasian state." Yet, shamelessly, they give the lengthy speeches in praise of the "Jewish state of Israel" as a "bastion of democracy."

To support their claim that Israel is a democracy, the Zionists point to the fact that there are some Arab representatives in the Israeli Parliament. What is not presented is the fact that these "Arabs" in the Israeli Parliament were elected not so much by the Arab community in Israel as Arabs, but by the Israeli Communist Party as Communists. Hence, they represent, not the Arabs, but the Communists of Israel. Other "Arabs" in the Israeli Parliament are affiliated with the ruling Mapai Party and vote in many cases against their own people, if so directed by the Party leadership. And at any rate, the Arabs of what is now Israel, are more entitled to participate in any form of government in their land even more than the European and other Jewish intruders into that land.

Furthermore, and in terms of democracy, the fact that there are some Arabs in the Parliament of the Jewish state, does not make the Jewish state a democracy any more than if in the

"Christian state of America" there were several Jewish representatives or in the "Caucasian state of America" there were some Negroes in its Senate. For democracy is more than the formalities of a parliament and elections and the existence of a few sample representatives of the various minority groups.

Democracy has been defined as that form of government which offers majority rule and minority rights. This "minority right" does not refer to the right of the minority to drink coffee or tea or to worship God, Jehovah, or Allah. This minority right means that the minority shall have at least the legal theoretical right to become a majority. However, a Jewish state by definition and by the very structure of its established order, sets up the Jews as a permanent majority and denies even the theoretical possibility of other minorities to ever become a majority. The concept of a permanent majority is a violation of the basic assumption of democracy which does not believe in any permanent majority. Hence, the non-Jews of the Jewish state of Israel are relegated to a position of a permanent minority status, a position written into the very structure of the state. This is by definition undemocratic.

Furthermore, there is no separation of chuch and state in Israel. This is not a mere theoretical academic issue. Under the British constitutional system, in theory the Queen is the head of the church and state much as she is in theory the commander of the armed forces and so on. But in Israel, the mixture between church and state is a reality which violates the basic assumption of democracy. For example, the questions of personal status (marriage, divorce, etc.) are subjected to religious but not civil courts. The Israeli state builds synagogues, but not churches or mosques, and assigns rabbis and pays their salaries. Under the rule of the Jewish Orthodoxy, marriage between Jews and non-Jews is forbidden. Such prohibition of marriage between Jews and non-Jews existed in Hitler's Nazi Germany and was abhorrent to the liberals. American "liberal" Jews should protest against this fascistic law of the Israeli state.

If there is any democracy in Israel, it is surely not for the Arab citizens who have been placed in the Jewish state in a position of permanent minority. As one Arab student at the Hebrew University stated recently, "For an Arab in Israel to be a citizen *and* proud, is impossible." Nor do all the Jewish citizens of Israel enjoy equality. There is discrimination by the European Jews against the oriental Jews. The senior editor of *Look* Magazine put it succinctly in a recent article entitled "Prejudice in Israel." The opening sentence of this article is revealing: "Israel is a testament to the inability of men to live together."[3]

Furthermore, and aside from this racial prejudice against oriental Jews, there is discrimination by the Orthodox Jews against the Reformed and Conservative Jews. The questions of personal status and religious performance having been entrusted to the Orthodoxy, the position of the Reformed and Conservative Jews in Israel is one of a discriminated minority. A Reformed rabbi is not permitted to officiate marriages nor does he have the freedom to conduct religious services as freely as the Orthodox rabbis do. The truth is that the American Jews enjoy a greater measure of civil and religious freedom in America than they would in the Jewish state of Israel. No wonder, then, that the American Jews, even though they talk about Israeli democracy, have refused singularly to go to its "haven."

There is no doubt that if in America civil marriage did not exist, and that marriage and divorce were subjected to religious laws, almost every American Jew would have raised a hubbub, objecting to such American laws. But the chanting about Israeli democracy goes on continuously, even if such undemocratic laws exist in Israel. Of course, the politicians' praise that Israel is a democracy is in the interest of getting the so-called "Jewish vote." I have even heard Chief Justice Earl Warren, whose commitment to the Jeffersonian principles regarding "the wall of separation between the church and state" is undeniable and who has taken that principle to its logical conclusion in the *Bible Reading* and other cases[4] — the same Earl Warren goes on unscrupulously to praise Israeli "democracy"! Evidently what is bad and forbidden in America will become permissible in Israel. These are two opposing standards to which I cannot subscribe, nor can any person with any measure of decency.

In this connection, I should like to say that while there are many Arabs who are courageous enough and have the decency to object to Arab dictatorship and autocracy, I have yet to see one decent Zionist Jew who would object to these undemocratic features in Israel. And we must admit that if the Arabs are not democratic, that will not make Israel a "bastion of democracy."

The Israeli "democracy" suffers yet from another point. Israel is almost a garrison state, and the powerful army of the little state has the ability to dictate much of the policies of the state in open violation of the democratic principle of civilian control over the military power. In the name of security, Israel has the strictest censorship over the press. According to The

New York Times, "All newspapers and periodicals published in Israel must be read before publication by a corps of young military officers assigned as censors. All dispatches of foreign correspondence must be submitted to the censors. All outgoing commercial cables are seen by the censors, and so is all film destined for public showing. All radio broadcasts must also be cleared."

The case of the two Israeli editors of the weekly *Bul* is a recent example of suppression of freedom of the press as done by a police state. Two editors, Shmuel Mor and Maxim Gilan, were "arrested, interrogated, indicted, tried, and sentenced," and nobody knew anything about the affair until some two months later when the shocking news was first revealed to an astonished and horrified world by The New York Times in New York.

Surely the two men had families and relatives, and as editors they had their colleagues and assistants and friends. And surely, these must have known of the disappearance of Messrs. Mor and Gilan. But none of these could raise the issue of the disappearance of these men, fearful of the Israeli secret police.

The suppression of the freedom of the press in itself is condemnable and undemocratic, but even more undemocratic and condemnable is the secret nature of the case. There is something basically wrong when two persons could be arrested, tried, sentenced, and imprisoned without anyone knowing or talking about the case, a case which everywhere else would be a public trial if not also a sensational affair. Such practices go on only in the police states, but not in a democracy.[5]

4. On Western Anti-Semitism and Persecution of the Jews.

It would go without saying that the atrocities committed against the Jews in the twentieth century in the West were more terrible than those committed by the barbarians or by primitive man. However, it should be recalled that Jewish persecution in Europe was the fault and the responsibility of Nazi Germany, not the Arabs. Many a westerner has developed a sense of guilt for what happened to the Jews in the West, and at western bloody hands. However, no westerner can relieve his sense of guilt by helping the poor Jews at the expense of the poor Arabs. Generosity to the Jews at the expense of the innocent Arabs is morally reprehensible and unacceptable to the Arabs or anyone else. The Arabs should not be expected to pay for the crimes of Hitler. Jewish persecution in Europe may vest the Jews who were persecuted in Europe with certain rights against Germany, but surely not against the Arabs.

The question of prejudice in the West is of utmost importance in this brief study, and we shall come back to the question of anti-Semitism and anti-Gentile-ism as the cause and effect for the present dangerous situation in the Middle East.

It should be noted here, however, that the question of anti-Semitism is primarily a western problem, and has never been part of the Middle East, its Arab or Islamic world.

Indeed, when the Jews in the West were persecuted in sixteenth century Spain, they were welcomed in Arab North Africa, and when in nineteenth century Russia, Jews were persecuted, they were welcomed in the Middle East. But the welcome extended to the persecuted Jews could not be offered to the Zionists who went into Palestine as a matter of "right," rather than a matter of grace, requesting the people of the area to provide them with refuge and shelter.

It was possibly the greatest mistake of Herzel when he stated in the First Zionist Congress that the establishment of the Jewish state should be based on right, and not on toleration. Surely, he misunderstood the nature of human beings, and evidently, he was totally ignorant of the Arabs, their attitude, psychology, history, and of the advent of Arab nationalism, which would not and could not reconcile itself with any such foreign intruding claim to rights to Palestine because of some whimsical historical connection.

5. *On Palestine Arab Resettlement*

One of the most insidious arguments advanced by the Zionists is that the Palestine Arab refugees should be resettled in places other than their homes. The Zionists maintain that the responsibility for the resettlement of the Arab refugees lies on the shoulders of the Arab leaders. This argument is of course based on the assumption that the Arab refugees are inanimate objects which could be moved and resettled at the whim of this Arab politician or the other. But the refugees are human beings with feelings and rights, and they are naturally determined to go home. The decision regarding their future is their own, and it is not up to Arab leaders.

This decision of the refugees to go home has been reported continuously by the United Nations Directors of UNRWA year after year, as well as by many impartial observers. The actual stubborn will of the refugees and their uncompromising attitude to return is today as strong, if not stronger, as it was nineteen years ago.

The Zionists offer generous constructive advice in terms of "Let's forget about the past and start from here." This is a blatant example of Zionist double standards. For while the entire Zionist claim to Palestine was based on the historical ground — namely, that Palestine belongs to the Jews because in the remote past of 2,000 years ago, certain Jews had conquered Palestine and the Jews have not forgotten Palestine over the past 2,000 years — the Zionists turn to the Arabs and ask them to forget about their land from which they were evicted only nineteen years ago! If the Zionists have not forgotten about Palestine despite the passing of 2,000 years, then it stands to reason that the Arabs cannot forget after only nineteen years about the homes in which they were born and raised. If the Zionists have not forgotten about Palestine for 2,000 years, the Arabs will not forget about it after 4,000 years. Let this be abundantly clear!

One of the wicked arguments advanced by the Zionists is that you cannot turn back the clock of history and permit the Arab refugees to go back to their homes. Alas! It was the Zionists who found, in the 2,000 years ago story, a logical ground to turn the clock of history back 2,000 years. There are then, according to the Zionists, two standards — one for the Zionists, and one for the non-Zionists — for sentimental attachments, rights, and behavior. The Zionists can turn back the clock of history 2,000 years, whereas the non-Zionists and Arabs should not attempt to turn it back a decade or two.

Many a Zionist Jew has claimed that the Jews are a "unique people" with unique rights and claims. This claim to "uniqueness" must be rejected totally by any self-respecting egalitarian person who is committed to the principle of equality of members of the human race. This question of "unique rights" of the "unique" Jews has been the cause of much of the problems of the Jews in the western societies and stimulates the creation of prejudice and counter prejudice: It led ultimately to the Hitler holocaust which in turn led to the establishment of the State of Israel. We shall come back to this question of "Jewish uniqueness" in a later chapter.

In connection with the question of historical rights, historical ties, and historical responsibility, it is in order here to note the recent resolutions of the Vatican Council. The Council resolved that the Jews of today are not responsible for whatever might have happened to Jesus at the hands of some Jews 2,000 years ago. This is only logical, reasonable, and it is high time and most gratifying that finally the Catholic Church has admitted this simple fact. Naturally, the Jews of today are not responsible for what happened 2,000 years ago. And, of course, by the same token, the Jews of today are not inheritors of Palestine because of a connection which existed 2,000 years ago.

Briefly, the Jews of today cannot disclaim responsibility and disadvantage that might be accrued from an historical tie to some past events, and claim an advantage that might be deduced from similar historic ties.

Unlike many Arabs, who have been opposed to the Vatican Council's resolution, I have welcomed the decision of the Council.

I believe that it is of paramount importance to note that the Jews of today are not responsible for the past any more than they can claim advantages because of past events. This point must be fully understood, if one would wish to see the establishment of peace in the Middle East and peace all over the world.

II
The Cause

Even though Herzl wrote THE JEWISH STATE, and in many quarters he is considered to be the Father of Zionism and Israel, the fact is that the true Father of Israel is Hitler even more than Herzl, and Israel is the product of anti-Semitism even more than of Zionism.

Indeed, if it were not due to Hitler and his barbarian behavior, Jews would not have rallied around Zionism, and would not have fled Europe to Palestine. All the attempts of the Zionist movement, its idealism, energy and devious means and devices, were unable to uproot the Jews from western countries to go to Palestine. Hitler succeeded where Herzl failed.

This brings us to the question of anti-Semitism, and we should recognize that it is anti-Semitism which is the ultimate cause of the conflict in the Middle East, and possible global war. We should therefore direct all our efforts toward the eradication of anti-Semitism and every form of prejudice directed toward anyone or any people on racial or religious grounds.

Briefly, anti-Semitism refers to the prejudice of the Gentiles toward the Jews. In modern times, it is more the product of Jewish emancipation in the West than the traditional religious bigotry. This has been supported by Herzl and has received the approval of Hannah Arendt and other scholars.

In 1966, a study conducted by the University of California on the question of CHRISTIAN BELIEFS AND ANTI-

SEMITISM was published. This study was financed by the Anti-Defamation League of B'nai Brith, which had offered the University of California a grant of half a million dollars. The study, conducted by Professors Charles Y. Glock and Rodney Stark, concludes, amongst other things, that conservatively, "at least one fourth of America's anti-Semites have a religious basis for their prejudice . . . . In terms of absolute numbers rather than percentage, these data indicate that approximately 17.5 million Americans who hold fairly strong anti-Semitic beliefs would also be classified [as religious bigots]. Far from being trivial, religious image of the modern Jew seems to lie at the root of anti-Semitism of millions of American adults."[6]

I believe that an adequate study of the question of prejudice and anti-Semitism could not be made by examining the Christian belief alone. It would seem that there are Jewish prejudices against the Christians as there are Christian prejudices against the Jews. Prejudice begets prejudice. It is a vicious circle in which it is hard to find the cause and the effect at the same time. Accordingly, I have coined the expression "anti-Gentile-ism" to refer to the prejudices of the Jews toward the Gentiles, much as anti-Semitism refers to the prejudices of the Gentiles toward the Jews.[7]

In June of 1966, the Action Committee on American-Arab Relations, of which I have the honor to be the Secretary-General, offered Columbia University a $100,000.00 grant to study the question of "Jewish Beliefs and Anti-Gentile-ism." The purpose of the study was to supplement the study by the University of California on "Christian Beliefs and Anti-Semitism," so that all causes and sources of prejudice could be studied in order to round out the entire issue.

The new expression, "anti-Gentile-ism," and the offer to Columbia to study its connection with Jewish beliefs is not an attempt to take issue with the Anti-Defamation League or to score points in a contest with that organization and with Zionism. That may be the endeavor of the Anti-Defamation League itself; our concern, however, is with a more serious question.

We are concerned with the question of prejudice which has led to wars, and we are interested in the elimination of prejudice, which is the road to peace. The long range purpose of this work on "Peace in the Middle East" is not only to undo what Hitler and Herzl had unfortunately created, or to the creation of which they had contributed. The long range purpose of this book is to find a means and a permanent solution to a basic human problem which includes, amongst other things, the so-called "Jewish question." Once the problem of prejudice is solved, permanent peace will be attained.

I have been extremely concerned with the question of anti-Semitism and anti-Gentile-ism, and so has been the Action Committee on American-Arab Relations. What is the reason for an American Arab organization to be interested in these issues, and why should it be so concerned with the problem to the point of offering $100,000.00 to an institution of higher learning to examine the question of prejudice? I shall give the answer to these questions later.

Presently, however, it is most important to note that the Anti-Defamation League, ostensibly concerned with the question of prejudice and its elimination, is not quite interested enough to work for the complete elimination of the disease of anti-Semitism. I suggest that, on the contrary, the Anti-Defamation League and other Zionist Jewish organizations are interested in retaining at least a mild form of anti-Semitism. Indeed, the Anti-Defamation League, the American Jewish Congress, and other Jewish organizations in America and elsewhere are committed to the preservation of a mild form of anti-Semitism, because these organizations are the beneficiaries of anti-Semitism today, and they would have no existence and their usefulness would end the moment anti-Semitism is eliminated.

Like all oligarchies which are concerned with the perpetuation of their power over the rank and file, the leaders of the various Zionist Jewish organizations are concerned with their own positions, even when these positions are diametrically opposed to the actual good of the rank and file in whose interest the organizations were supposedly formed.

The Jewish organizations which are concerned with Israel and are dedicated to its support are today the beneficiaries of anti-Semitism much as Israel itself is a by-product of anti-Semitism.

The fact is that the Father of Israel is none other than the greatest anti-Semite of all time. Put in the proper historical context, the real Father of Israel is Hitler rather than Herzl, and the state is the creation of anti-Semitism rather than Zionism. There would have been no Israel if there were no Hitler and no anti-Semitism, and most likely there will be no Israel when anti-Semitism ceases to exist.

Our task to bring peace to the Middle East therefore is predicated on eliminating anti-Semitism, and hence, our efforts should be directed toward that problem.

It is one of the ironies of life that while the various Jewish organizations have been living off, and have been the beneficiaries of, anti-Semitism, the real victims of anti-Semitism at present are the Arabs. More specifically, the real victims are the Palestinian Arabs who have lost their homes and land, which have been occupied by the European Jews, who were once the victims of western anti-Semitism.

We are therefore deeply committed to the elimination of prejudice, not only because prejudice is a form of disease that degrades the human being — the one who entertains prejudice even more than the person against whom prejudice is directed — but also because it will lead to war. Because the Arabs are today the indirect victims of western prejudice, and because they will never accept their present position of being the victims of anti-Semitism and Zionism, the situation in the Middle East is frought with danger, which might lead to a global conflict.

Our task is to prevent the possibilities of war from becoming a reality, and to eliminate the injustices inflicted upon the Arabs by the Zionists, as well as to provide the best of opportunities for those Jews who were victims of western prejudice and anti-Semitism.

In this spirit, I am dedicating this effort to the young liberals and intellectuals of the world, who are humanist enough to be opposed to prejudice and believe in the equality of man, and who are idealist enough to call a spade a spade and oppose bigotry whether it stems from the white or the Negro, from the Jews or the Gentiles, from the religious zealot or the atheist, notwithstanding the political consequences that may occur as a result of such stands. For the goal of eliminating prejudice and preventing war represents the greatest challenge to the young idealists and intelligentsia everywhere.

I have said that the Anti-Defamation League and other Zionist Jewish organizations are interested in perpetuating a mild form of anti-Semitism and that they are not genuinely interested in eliminating that disease. To be sure, the Anti-Defamation League does conduct studies, hold seminars on the question of prejudice, and to an extent, that would lead to the elimination of anti-Semitism. However, its picking on the Christians, irking them, and continuously insinuating that prejudice is a one-way street, are activities of the League which will create resentment and perpetuate prejudice and stimulate anti-Semitism. Furthermore, the failure of the Anti-Defamation League to offer Jewish beliefs and tradition for examination by a university, much as the League had asked the University of California to examine Christian beliefs and tradition, would tend to strengthen the feelings of many that the League is only concerned with prejudice when it stems from Christian beliefs and not concerned with prejudice when it stems from Jewish beliefs. Or does the Anti-Defamation League claim that no Jew has any prejudice toward the Gentiles?

I believe that anti-Semitism could not be eliminated without the elimination of anti-Gentile-ism at the same time. As long as the Anti-Defamation League and others are not willing to eliminate anti-Gentile-ism, or at least to examine the question of anti-Gentile-ism, it is not possible to see the end of anti-Semitism. That, of course, is exactly what the Anti-Defamation League would wish to see and to retain. It is for this reason that we appeal to liberal Jews, young and old, who are genuinely concerned with the question of prejudice, and who are willing to eliminate Jewish prejudice as well as Gentile prejudice. I appeal to the young liberals to take issue with the leadership of the various Jewish organizations and to call their leaders to task. The young Jews should ask the leaders of the Jewish organizations to adopt one standard of morality and behavior. They should be against prejudice from whatever source prejudice might stem.

III

Anti-Semitism and Anti-Gentile-ism

The often used expression, "anti-Semitism," has come to refer to the prejudices of the Gentiles toward the Jews, even if ethnically the overwhelming majority of the Jews of today are not Semites. The Jews of today are ethnically of various backgrounds, and only Yemenite Jews might be properly considered Semites. The fact is that the Arabs are more Semite than David Ben-Gurion, Golda Meir, Levy Eshkol, Will Maslow, Arnold Forster, and others who are most likely of Slavic ethnic background.

If the majority of world Jews are not Semites, then the expression "anti-Semitism" could not properly refer to them. But the expression has been continuously employed, and under present usage, it does refer to the prejudices of the Gentiles toward the Jews. This fact, however, is not as important as the premise behind the continued use of the term. The continued employment of the expression "anti-Semitism" assumes that prejudice is a one-way street: that for some reason or another (the University of California study attempted to find the reasons which stem from Christian beliefs) the non-Jews as a whole dislike or hate or have prejudices against the Jews as a whole. The assumption behind this thinking and this use of the expression "anti-Semitism" is a one-sided assumption. The correct analysis would provide the valid postulate and the posture — namely, that prejudice is a two-way street. That is to say, there is anti-Semitism because there is anti-Gentile-ism, and there is anti-Gentile-ism because there is anti-Semitism. It is a vicious circle. Whatever the original cause and wherever the beginning of the vicious circle, there is no doubt that anti-Semitism is as bad as anti-Gentile-ism, and anti-Gentile-ism is as bad as anti-Semitism.

It is to be noted that anti-Semitism is a western phenomenon. Whatever political and economic implications it may have today, its original roots might be found in religious schism. When Christianity evolved out of Judaism, to the original Jews, the Christians were deviates and renegades, much as to the new Christians, the Jews had deliberately failed to accept the new teachings.

Worse than the traditional animosity arising between the deviates and the orthodoxy, was the fact that each group claimed to have "The Truth" and to follow "The Road to Salvation." To the Jews, the Torah was the truth and the path; to the Christians, the road to salvation was through the person of Jesus Christ. Moreover, each group claimed to have a status of "chosen people." Originally, to the Jews, the concept stemmed from tribalistic feelings and ties, and later it meant that God had chosen the Jews to deliver His Message. To the newly found religion, however, the Christian Church and membership in the Church provided the status of chosen people. The animosity and the conflict between the two concepts of chosen people resembled the conflict between the church and state in the West.[8]

The conflict between church and state arose from the fact that each claimed complete authority and demanded absolute loyalty from the people.[9] This conflict was eventually resolved after the bloody years of the Reformation and the wars which ultimately created the modern state. We may be too close to the events, but it is possible that the conflict between the two concepts of "chosen people" in the West has been resolved or is on the way to being resolved as a result of the inhumane behavior of Nazi Germany and the German atrocities against the Jews. In the case of the conflict between church and state, the solution came as a result of the accommodation between the two domains to each other's claim. The Church was recognized as the authority in the spiritual field, and the state in the temporal realm.

The conflict between the chosen people concepts may be resolved as a result of the process of de-tribalization, in which the human *individual* of whatever "chosen people" group may become the standard of judgement, blamed or praised, rather than the *group* to which he belongs. Only if man's efforts are directed toward this goal of individualization and de-tribalization might the conflict between the various "chosen peoples" gradually wither away. The human race will then have "chosen individuals," of whom the whole of mankind can be proud, and no more "chosen peoples" who can cause resentment and lead to conflicts.

Accordingly, all efforts should be directed toward the de-tribalization process and internationalization. In the midst of this stream, any trend toward strengthening tribalistic ties of nationalism is contrary to the trend of modern history and the good of the individual human beings concerned. It is therefore regrettable that Zionism has appeared on the horizon at this stage of human development as a reactionary force contrary

– 43 –

to the new trend of human history.[10]

* * *

The Anti-Defamation League had offered the University of California a half a million dollar grant to study the question of "Christian Beliefs and Anti-Semitism." I have suggested that it would not be possible to understand the complex question of prejudice and all roots of that problem by examining Christian beliefs alone. I have suggested that Jewish beliefs and tradition should likewise be examined and studied. There is at least sufficient evidence to warrant such an investigation. The Action Committee on American-Arab Relations has offered Columbia University a grant to conduct a study on the question to find out whether there are elements in Jewish beliefs and tradition which might lead to prejudice against the Gentiles. If so, such elements should be removed, eliminated, or at least explained in new terms to stamp out Jewish prejudice, much as today the Jews are, understandably and legitimately, calling upon the Christians to eliminate from Christian belief and tradition what might lead to prejudice against the Jews.

Concerned as we have been with the problem of prejudice, and knowing that the Anti-Defamation League was equally concerned with the problem, the Action Committee on American-Arab Relations invited the Anti-Defamation League to cooperate in a joint sponsorship of the study to be conducted by Columbia University. Likewise, the cooperation and support of the National Conference of Christians and Jews was solicited. It was hoped that these organizations would participate in the cooperative effort to eliminate all sources of prejudice.

Unfortunately, the response of the Anti-Defamation League was negative. Its one sentence reply said discourteously and abruptly, "Be advised that the Anti-Defamation League is not at all interested in any cooperative effort with you or your organization." This abrupt and rather discourteous response was discouraging and astonishing. It was a most intolerant attitude exhibited by an organization which asks for tolerance and calls for understanding. The reply of the National Conference of Christians and Jews was equally negative.

Whether these organizations believe that the Jews have no prejudice against the Gentiles and therefore there is no need to study what does not exist, or whether these organizations assume that prejudice is a one-way street and while it is permissible to pick on the Christians and demand that the Christians cleanse their religion, there is no need to make a similar demand of the Jews, it is most unfortunate that they have failed to cooperate and express their interest in the proposed study

We have suggested that the Anti-Defamation League is not genuinely interested in the elimination of anti-Semitism, and that it would indeed wish to retain at least a mild form of that "-ism." The reply of the League and its attitude confirmed the validity of our suggestion. Likewise, and with much regret, Columbia University has failed to accept the grant of the Action Committee on American-Arab Relations, and undoubtedly as a result of the pressure of the Zionist Jews, who wish to retain anti-Semitism rather than work toward its elimination. Because of the Zionist desire to retain anti-Semitism, the great University unwittingly is now acting in collusion with the Zionists to perpetuate anti-Semitism rather than embark upon a project which might lead to the final elimination of that disease. It is rather insulting to the sensitive that the University of California should undertake a study on the question of prejudice as it stems from Christian beliefs, and Columbia University fails to accept a project to study prejudice as it might stem from Jewish beliefs. Does this mean that the Jews, or at least some of them, have no prejudice toward the Gentiles?

I suggest that there is at least sufficient ground to prove the existence of anti-Gentile-ism. While this book cannot examine that question at length, it is in order to present some evidence in support of the allegation. I shall consider some of the sources which lead to prejudice and counter-prejudice: the terms anti-Semitism and anti-Gentile-ism being both sides of the same coin in many instances.

We must be fair and objective enough to admit the simple fact that all religions, having as a primary desire to attract their adherents to their own virtue, do have factors and elements which might be prejudicial toward other religions. If this is true of Christian beliefs, it is likewise true of Jewish beliefs. It is also true of Islam, even though to a lesser extent.[11]

There are many Jewish religious teachings and practices with elements which might lead to prejudice toward the non-Jews, and the understanding or genuine misunderstanding by the non-Jews of such Jewish teachings might lead to prejudice and counter-prejudice on the part of the non-Jews toward the Jews and on the part of the Jews toward the non-Jews. Hence, there is a definite need to clear up the confusion which might lead to misunderstanding and stimulate prejudice as a result of such teachings.

Take, for example, the famous Kol Nidre, the prayer which is recited by the Jews three times at the beginning of Yom Kippur services. This has been the cause of many problems and much confusion, prejudice and counter-prejudice. The text of the Kol Nidre reads as follows:

> All vows, obligations, oaths, and anathemas, whether called "konam," "konas," or by any other name, which we may vow or swear or pledge, or whereby we may be bound, from this Day of Atonement until the next (whose happy coming we await), we do repent. May they be deemed absolved, forgiven, annulled, and void and made of no effect; they shall not bind us nor have power over us. The vows shall not be reckoned vows; the obligations shall not be obligatory, nor the oaths be oaths.[12]

When one reads this text, and particularly the broad scope of the opening phrase, "All vows, obligations, oaths, etc. . . . may they be annulled and void and made of no effect," any reasonable man will naturally be offended and will believe that the oath of a Jew cannot be trusted, as the Jews consider themselves absolved of responsibility of such promises and oaths.

However, upon studying the Jewish Encyclopedia and other Jewish scholarly efforts, one will find that the Kol Nidre refers, not really to all vows, but only to special vows. As one authority puts it, the Kol Nidre only cancels "all forced or harmful personal vows."[13]

Of course, not all people would bother to study the Jewish Encyclopedia and Jewish scholarly works to learn that the Kol Nidre refers only to personal vows. To the multitude of the Gentiles, the Kol Nidre is *prima facie* incriminating, and understandably so!

The Jewish Encyclopedia says that the Kol Nidre ". . . has been one of the means used by Jewish apostites and by enemies of the Jews to cast suspicion on the trustworthiness of an oath taken by a Jew." It goes on to say, however, that some Jews have misused the Kol Nidre and it cannot be denied that ". . . an unscrupulous man might think it offers a means of escape from the obligations and promises which he had assumed and made. . . ." The Kol Nidre, according to the Jewish Encyclopedia, is not a part of the teachings of the Jewish religion and it refers only to oaths taken which do not affect others. Nevertheless, ". . . many ignorant persons believe that all their vows and oaths are annulled through this formula, and consequently, they take such obligations upon themselves carelessly."[14]

To the extent that some unscrupulous Jews and ignorant individuals amongst them believe that the formula provides them with an escape clause from the vows they take in regard to others, such a belief is based on an assumption that it is permissible for the Jews to take advantage of the non-Jews. Somehow, it would assume that the non-Jews are not quite equal and that what is fair for the Jews to do is not permitted in the case of others. If this stems from prejudice in the minds of the Jews toward the non-Jews, it will also create prejudice in the minds of the non-Jews toward the Jews.

To eliminate much of this confusion and anti-Gentile-ism and anti-Semitism, I suggest that Jewish theologians and others concerned should attempt to correct the situation and eliminate the confusion and prejudices which the Kol Nidre stimulates. I suggest that Jewish thinkers have an obligation to correct this, much as they want Christians to correct and eliminate from Christianity whatever might stimulate prejudice toward the Jews. The Jewish theologians and thinkers can do this by inserting at the opening of the Kol Nidre prayer one word. It would accordingly read, "All *personal* vows, etc. . . . may they be annulled, etc. . . ."

Someone may object that the Jews do not have a hierarchy authorized to add to and change and amend their religion. This may or may not be the case. At any rate, if our purpose is to eliminate prejudice and live in a better world of tomorrow, then it is of utmost importance to create such authorities or somehow devise a legal means to amend such prayers which do create unnecessary misunderstanding and harm. If the old forms have been harmful or led to prejudice, and if we want a prejudice-free world, then we must change the old forms and formulae or at least reinterpret them to meet the new expectations. It is not possible to wish for the elimination of prejudice which has been the result of previous formulae and retain the old forms.[15]

In addition to the actual teachings and the written words, it seems that, due to persecution or because of the belief in the concept of the "chosen people," many Jews have developed a complex as a result of which they feel that they are always given the "raw end of the deal" and therefore, in order to make up for the disadvantages (real or imagined), they deserve, and are entitled, in the name of fairness, to take advantage of the non-Jews.

This is usually the psychology of all minorities who feel persecuted. But if it is correct that many Jews do believe that it is permissible for them to do what may not be permissible for others (because the Jews had been mistreated, or for any other reason), then it must be made clear that to make up for the persecution of some Jews by some non-Jews, the Jews are not entitled to take the law into their own hands and assume for themselves what is not permitted for others. To oppose prejudice and persecution, one should not, as many Jews have, develop a feeling of counter-prejudice, directed in many cases toward individuals and people who have had no prejudice toward the Jews to begin with.

The problem with prejudice is not that retaliatory actions are taken by the victim against the guilty. The problem is that a victim may take retaliatory action against people who are not guilty, but only in some vague way or another might be associated with the guilty person. It is a pre-judgement against a whole people, attributing to them a collective responsibility, where in truth, the responsibility should be an individual one, assumed by the guilty person toward whom the victim of prejudice should direct his feelings.

The psychological commitment to the concept of the "chosen people" breeds prejudice and counter-prejudice. This, in my opinion, is at the root of both anti-Semitism and anti-Gentile-ism.

Also related to this concept is the allegation that the Jews are a "unique people."

I suggest that the Jews are neither unique nor un-unique. If they are unique, then the Christians are unique and the Moslems are unique and the Buddhists are unique, and so on. It is indeed insulting and shameful that many Jews hold to this myth. In that they are no different than an Adolph Hitler who believed in the uniqueness of the Aryan people. If there is anything unique about the Jews, it is that they are members of the human race.

What is so unique about one Murray Hyman, a filthy little thief, who also happens to be a Jew? If there is anything unique about him, it is that he is a little thief, and a crook. Accordingly, I suggest that while there are no chosen people and no unique people, there might be, of course, unique individuals. And these are unique not because they are Jews or Christians or Moslems or Buddhists, nor because they are Americans or Russians or Arabs or Englishmen, but because they are individuals under certain socio-economic conditions, and have been able to unfold the gifts which have been given to them by God or nature. Such individuals are a source of pride to the human race, even though "unique peoples" are sources of prejudice, conflict, and wars, to the detriment of all people.

There are many who say that the Jews are "smart." I believe, while *some* Jews are indeed very bright, there are many Jews who are very stupid. True, there are individual bright Jews. However, it seems that as a collectivity the Jews have been a failure, if adaptation to environment is a sign of success. But then, of course, it is true that many Jews have been able to adapt to the various environments throughout the centuries and in the various fields in modern times. Nevertheless, the so-called adaptation has been an awkward one, continuously creating prejudice, and ill effect.

At any rate, one of the most stupid collective actions in recent times of the majority of the Jews has been their espousing of Zionism. With hopes to solve the "Jewish question," modern Zionism has not only failed to solve the Jewish question, but has also created an Arab question. Furthermore, it has created the problem of double loyalty of the Jews, and has created the problem of tension between the Jews in Israel and the Jews in the *Diaspora*. Israeli Jews look down on the renegade Jews in America and elsewhere who willfully have failed to obey the first commandment of Zionism, namely to go home after two thousand years![16]

Deduced from the allegation of "Jewish uniqueness" is the proposition that the Jews as a rule may want "to have their cake and eat it, too." Of course, if this is true, it is deplorable, even though it might be understandable. As a matter of fact, there are many Jews who wish to be both nationalists and internationalists, a religious group and a tribal-racial group, committed to universalism, yet following a clannish kind of behavior. In these, the Jews are like the rest of mankind no more and no less.

However, while large segments of people everywhere are coming out of their specific little shells to become members of the human race, many of the Jews are building the shell around them and strengthening the walls. It is the reactionary nature and a trend contrary to the pattern of human behavior of the present day that further leads to prejudice as it irks people and annoys the sensitive.

For in the era of internationalism and the triumph of the human individual, it is one of the annoying factors when Jewish nationalists endeavor to somehow trace themselves to Palestine and to Abraham. Many a Jew of eastern European origin is ethnically 100% eastern European Slav, yet he claims racial and ethnic ties to Palestine. If one of them might have 1% or 5% of Semitic blood, it would indeed be a case of dogmatic racism when he maintains that the 1% or 5% of Semitic blood overrules and overshadows the 99% or 95% of the Slavic blood he might have.

This feeling that the 1% might overrule the 99% is illogical, dogmatic, shameful, racial, and utterly preposterous. It is the same mentality of the Nazi, possibly a bit worse, and in reverse.

I maintain that the concept of the "chosen people" or the unique people is a myth, and indeed a dangerous myth at that. Simon Dubnow has written extensively on the significance of

Jewish history, its uniqueness and so on. I suggest that the only significant unique aspect of Jewish history is that the Jews are a part of the human race and human history. This is both the most significant aspect of the Jews and at the same time so very universal that it makes the uniqueness a tribute to human history and the human race, rather than the Jewish history and the Jews.

The Jews have to become a part of the human race, even before being Jews. This observation is directed of course to those Jews who are first Jews and then members of the human race. However, there are others who are first human beings and in the second place, Jews. There are many such Jews and to these universalist men of good will and genuine intention, I direct my appeal.

I appeal to the members of the American Jewish Committee, to Jewish thinkers, philosophers, and intellectuals to repudiate the myth of the chosen people and the myth of Jewish uniqueness. These myths have been the cause of prejudice and counter-prejudice, and if we are embarking upon a life free from prejudice, such concepts should be repudiated and otherwise made known to all parties that they are insignificant and empty legacies of the past, and while they might have some theoretical academic historic interest, they have no validity or place at present as factors in human relationships.

To eliminate anti-Semitism, then, such features of anti-Gentile-ism must also be eliminated.

I believe that the reformers, the liberals, the educators, and all concerned, should direct their efforts toward eradicating the two obnoxious "-isms" at the same time. Any attempt at eradicating anti-Semitism and forgetting about anti-Gentile-ism is incomplete and is therefore doomed to failure. At present, while thoughtful and liberal Gentiles are attempting to educate the Gentiles and provide them with the proper attitude toward the Jews, liberal and thoughtful Jews should educate the Jews to eliminate their prejudices toward the Gentiles. It is only then that educational efforts at eliminating prejudice would be successful.

Furthermore, and much as at present the Christian churches are attempting to remove from Christian literature and theology any anti-Jewish references which might lead to prejudice against the Jews, it is the obligation of Jewish theologians and rabbis and thinkers to remove from Jewish literature and theology any anti-Christian or anti-Gentile references which might lead to prejudice against the Gentiles.

Of course, not all Jews have anti-Gentile prejudices, any more than all the Christians are anti-Semites. However, many of the Jews do have anti-Gentile prejudices, and to the extent that these prejudices stem from Jewish beliefs and tradition, liberal and thoughtful Jews should direct their efforts toward the elimination of such anti-Gentile prejudices much as thoughtful and liberal Christians are attempting to remove from Christian beliefs and tradition what may lead to anti-Jewish prejudice. It is then that we shall live in a prejudice free world.

IV

The Solution

When Israel was established in 1948, it was thought in many quarters in the West that the new state would be a source of stability and progress in the Middle East and that the Arabs would sooner or later come to accept its existence.

Today, some nineteen years have elapsed, and the Arabs are as uncompromising as they were before. Those familiar with the history of the Middle East and the psychology of the Arabs and indeed with human psychology *per se,* will recognize that the Arabs will never accept the European Jews in Palestine any more than they accepted the European Crusaders when they invaded the Middle East or the heathen Europeans of the time of Alexander the Great. Likewise, of course, the Arabs fought against the foreign Moslem Turks of the Ottoman Empire who had ruled their land for many years. In Algeria, the Arabs fought against the French, who had established themselves there for some one hundred thirty years, until the French were expelled from the area. Accordingly, and if there is a definite desire for peace and a desire to avoid a global war, a *new* approach to the problem of the Middle East is in order.

On May 21st, 1965, the Action Committee on American-Arab Relations proposed its Peaceful Solution to the problem in the Middle East. This proposal takes into consideration the actual welfare of the human individuals involved in the conflict as it looks to the establishment of peace in the area. It calls for a gradual return to normalcy and a peaceful elimination of the cause of the conflict in Palestine.

The ultimate purpose is to establish peace and reverse by 1984 the events of 1948. In 1948, Palestine was violently changed into Israel, causing much bloodshed and displacing and expelling the people of Palestine. In 1984, we wish to turn Israel peacefully into Palestine and provide the best of opportunities and life for the European Jews who were forced to go to Palestine under complex circumstances.

To that end, we are cailing for opportunities to be provided for the Jews, now in Israel, to return to their countries of origin or immigrate to countries of their choice. More specifically, we are calling for the admission of one million Israeli Jews to North America over a period of some twenty years. These are primarily the European Jews who were displaced in Europe and went, under the pressure of terrible circumstances, to Palestine and caused the displacement of the Arabs. A gradual and normal pattern of immigration of these to North America will be in the usual tradition of European immigration to these shores.

As an integral part of the proposal, we are calling upon the Arab governments to provide prompt and adequate compensation to the Jews for the property they own and leave behind. Likewise, we are calling upon the Arab governments to admit their former citizens, the Arab Jews, to their countries of origin and accord them with their proper rights and dignity and positions.

Furthermore, we maintain that all the Jews who might wish to stay in the Holy Land for purely religious purposes should stay there along with all the Christians and Moslems. The number of Jews who qualify on this basis to stay in the Holy

Land is no more than ten per cent of the present Israeli population.

We believe that large segments of the Israeli Jews of European origin would be interested to immigrate to North America and Australia or return to western Europe. Others may wish to immigrate to South America and other places of their choice. By 1967, there have been more than 180,000 Israeli Jews who left Israel and went to Canada, the United States, and many of them returned to western Europe, including Germany.

The majority of world Jews have chosen, by their own free will, America as their homeland. The American Jews have stubbornly declined the "opportunity" to go to Israel, despite Zionist endeavors. Indeed, the fact is that large majorities of the Israeli Jews, particularly those of European origin, would also choose America as their homeland, if given the opportunity.

I believe that large segments of the Israeli Jews would opt to leave Israel if given the opportunity for the following reasons:

There is a greater abundance of opportunity in North America than in Israel. Furthermore, the European Jews, being westerners by tradition and heritage, find themselves foreigners in the large ghetto of Israel amongst an ever-expanding oriental Jewish population. And thirdly, because there is a moral crisis in the heart and mind of many a sensitive Jew, now in Israel, knowing that the land and soil under his feet belong to the Palestinian Arab who is now in a refugee camp across the border. The sensitive Jew is plagued not only by the moral crisis, but he also knows full well that the Arab refugees some day will go back to their homes and land forcefully, if not permitted to return peacefully.

Accordingly, many sensitive Israeli Jews would resolve the

moral crisis in favor of a peaceful departure from Palestine, should they find the opportunity and ways and means to do so.

In this connection one might ask: Do Israeli Jews today have the right to leave Israel? The answer is the Jews of Israel have the legal right to leave. But there are basic economic obstacles. When the concentration camps were opened after World War II in Europe, the first choice of the Displaced Persons was to immigrate to America. However, Zionist organizations, ostensibly concerned with the welfare of the Jewish D.P.'s, literally "forced" these desperate people to go to Palestine by offering them financial support and other assistance if they opted to go there, and deny them any help if they chose to immigrate to America or any place else. The Zionist leaders were not concerned with the individual Jews and their actual good and right to exercise their free will and make their own choice. The concern of the Zionists was to build a state and in that process they sacrificed the individual and subordinated his welfare to the goal of establishing the state.

At present, however, and as the result, if any Jew wishes to leave the State of Israel, he is obliged to return to the Jewish Agency all the expenditures spent on him, including travel, housing, rehabilitation, etc. Assuming the total expenditure was $5,000.00, and assuming, according to the best estimate, that the annual income of the person is between $750.00 and $900.00, it is evident that an Israeli Jew who may wish to leave Israel will be unable to return the amount spent on him when he was taken to Israel, except after many many years. Hence, he is a sort of state-held prisoner and therefore not "free" to emigrate.

Accordingly, if the Israeli Jews are to leave, they should be provided with real opportunity to enable them to exercise their free will and depart.

But who can provide the *opportunity* for those Israeli Jews who are searching for a better life elsewhere? I believe the responsibility lies on the shoulders of the American Jews, Zionists and non-Zionists. This indeed is the *greatest challenge and opportunity for the American Jewry to provide the opportunities for the Israeli Jews who might wish to depart.*

I suggest that the American Jews have the moral obligation to provide this opportunity for their fellow Jews who may wish to leave Israel, much as American Jews provided the means for the European Jews to go to Palestine and provided the finances for the uprooting of other Jewish communities to go there. The American Jews likewise have the financial ability to provide the opportunity for their fellow Jews who may wish to depart from Israel to go to various countries of their choice. Finally, American Jews have the legal right, under the 1966 Immigration Law, to invite their relatives and kin to immigrate to America.

This is the greatest opportunity the American Jews have to work for peace and the good of their fellow Jews. This opportunity, however, is predicated upon the assumption that the American Jews are *indeed interested in peace and are indeed interested in the actual good and welfare of their fellow Jews.*

This Peace Proposal has been submitted to the United States Department of State and was presented to the American Jewish Committee as well as to the United Nations. The Proposal has received the wide support of various prominent individuals and the endorsement of many humanitarian and peace organizations. It has, however, received opposition from two quarters: First, the anti-Semites who do not like Jews and do not wish to have more Jews in the United States and in the West. And, second, strange as it may seem, the Peace Proposal has received the opposition of some unscrupulous Zionist Jewish leaders.

To the anti-Semites and the conservatives, I wish to say that our Proposal for providing opportunities for the return of the Jews to countries of western Europe and North America, at worst, is the best solution from any angle. Should the present situation in the Middle East continue, America may be involved in another Vietnam-like conflict in the Middle East. Today, American boys are being killed in Vietnam, thousands of miles away from home. I fear that American boys might someday be engaged in killing people and being killed thousands of miles away from home — in the Middle East. Whether such American involvement would be in the interest of the foreign state of Israel or on behalf of the Arabs of Palestine, it is equally dangerous. For involvement in the conflict there will be detrimental to America, to the Arabs, as well as to the Jews, and a threat to world peace.

The Peace Proposal contemplates that the solution to the problem of Palestine will be achieved by 1984. By that time the population of the United States will be some 250 million. Under these circumstances, the admission of some half million Israeli Jews of European origin to the United States and the admission of another half million to Canada, will not affect the general composition of North American society.

I wish to address a word or two to those who do not like Jews. Please remember that the Jews are members of the human race and are individuals and as such there are good Jews and bad Jews just as there are good Christians and bad Christians, and good Moslems and bad Moslems. You cannot get rid of

the Jews and must learn to live with this fact, even if you may
not wish to live with any particular Jewish person. Of course,
those Jews who feel that they are first Jews and then members
of the human race must also learn the correct order of things,
if our appeal to those prejudiced against the Jews should be
fruitful.

As a footnote and a secondary advantage of the Peace Proposal, we should note that the solution proposed will eliminate
once and for all the problem of American Jews raising hundreds
of millions of dollars and syphoning it into the foreign state
of Israel. The present day threat to the security of the dollar
and dollar drain will, to a good extent, be diminished. This
also should be of interest to the conservative elements, who
should welcome our Peace Proposal despite their feelings on
other grounds. Of course, the solution proposed will also end
the continuous taxes imposed on the American Jewish community by the Zionists in the interest of a foreign state. This taxa-
tion without representation will end and its termination will be
in the interest of the American Jewish community itself.

As for the opposition to the Peace Proposal by the unscrupulous Zionist leaders, and other selfish Jews who wish to have
the good life for themselves in western societies and in America,
and deny it to their fellow Jews, this is most unfortunate, and
it is an expression of the double standards practiced among Zionist Jews themselves. For example, Rabbi Joachim Prinz, a Jew
from Berlin who came to the United States and is now enjoying
life in this country as an American citizen, is so selfish and
thoughtless that while he wishes to have the good life for himself here, he would deny it to his former German Jewish
colleagues who had gone, under the pressure of the events of

the time, to Palestine. Prinz, the selfish man, opposes the admission of his friends to the United States.

It is for this reason that I appeal to the rank and file members of the American Jewish community. I appeal over the heads of their so-called leaders, requesting the rank and file to challenge the selfish leaders and consider the actual interest of the human individual co-religionist and fellow Jew. In this spirit, I appeal to them to invite their relatives, now in Israel, to immigrate to North America and offer them the opportunity to go to countries of their choice.

Indeed, I believe that both the Israeli and Arab governments have been unable to solve the problem, and hence, I appeal over the heads of the governments to the individuals to do their share on behalf of peace in the Middle East. If our concern is with the individual and his actual welfare, rather than the worship of a state — and the progress of human civilization seems to indicate a trend toward the de-tribalization of the individual and his triumph over the tribe and the group — then it is in order to appeal to the individuals to do their share on behalf of peace and on behalf of the actual welfare of fellow human individuals involved in a dilemma which may lead to global destruction.

It has been argued that Jews coming to America may find freedom and prosperity in this country, but the question of security for the Jews will be left unanswered. It has been suggested that the psychological security of the Jews is linked with Israel. This argument is fallacious and most insulting. It is not correct to say that the American Jews are secure because of Israel; the security of Israel itself depends on America. To say that Ambassador Arthur J. Goldberg, representing the United

States of America, is secure because of Ambassador Michael S. Comay of Israel, is an insult in addition to being absurd.

American Jews are secure because they are Americans and members of a free society, dedicated to the proposition that men are equal regardless of their race, religion, and national origin. It is the free society of America which provides protection for America Jews as well as for Americans of other backgrounds. If a Hitler should raise his ugly head in America, and were to put American Jews in concentration camps and prevent them from leaving the United States, no Israel could do anything whatsoever against such a movement any more than Japan, which was by far more powerful than Israel, was able to do anything on behalf of the American Japanese who were placed in relocation centers during the Second World War.

To be sure, there are today in America, as well as in other parts of the West, cases of anti-Semitism. But this problem should be resolved here, much as discrimination against the Negroes should be eliminated here in America, rather than eliminating it by sending the American Negroes to Africa. Accordingly, the claim that Israel is solving the "Jewish problem" or that it will provide a haven to which the Jews could go in time of trouble, or that Israel provides psychological security for the Jews — such claims do not stand the test of rigorous analysis.

Today, American Jews can go to Israel because of American laws permitting them to go, *not* because of Israel itself. Zionism, accordingly, has failed to solve the so-called Jewish question, and hence, there is a need for a newer approach. The approach suggested by the Action Committee on American-Arab Relations should be thoroughly examined by all concerned with peace and human dignity, as this Proposal provides the way out of the dilemma.

I believe that the rank and file Jews in America as well as in Israel will support in general our Proposal for Peace. Unfortunately, the Zionist and Israeli leaders, being members of the oligarchy and having vested interest as members of the Establishment, are concerned with their own selfish interest rather than the actual good of the rank and file members on whose behalf the Establishment was supposedly set up in the beginning. But I have faith in the individuals to revolt in the long run against the oligarchies and members of the vested interest.

I have suggested that all the Jews who may wish to stay in the Holy Land for purely religious purposes should be allowed to stay there along with all the Christians and Moslems. The Holy Land should become the religious capital of the world, rather than the political center of the New York Zionist Jews. Such a solution will satisfy the religious sentiments of those Jews who find some sentimental ties to that region, much as it will satisfy the sentimental ties of the Christians as well as the Moslems to the Holy Land.

With regard to the question of Jewish repatriation to their countries of origin or immigration to countries of their choice, as suggested by the Action Committee on American-Arab Relations, some questions have been raised. One is that the European Jews were so desperate during Hitler's days that they had to go somewhere and Palestine was that place. It is argued that the human person has his first commitment and obligation to his life, and in the interest of the preservation of that life, he might step on someone else's private property. According to this argument, it was unfortunate and regrettably unavoidable that European Jews, attempting to escape the horror of Hitler, were forced to step on the private rights of Palestinian Arabs.

I think that this argument has a great deal of validity. But we must add that such desperate circumstances and commitment to life preservation will confer only a temporary moral right of the trespasser over the private rights of others. Accordingly, the Jews who had to flee Hitler's Europe might claim a moral right to stay temporarily in Palestine, but surely they cannot claim any moral right to stay there permanently. Of course, it is a matter of fact that the Jews of Europe went to Palestine not only as the persecuted who begged for a refuge, but as a matter of historic "right," as claimed by the Zionists. This claim to right could not be admitted. And even if we admit the moral principle of "temporary stay" when one is fleeing an insane criminal who is threatening him with death, the right to "permanent stay" has not been and could not be admitted.

It has also been argued that the Jews now in Israel have no place to which to return even if the French in Algeria were able to leave Algeria and go back to France. I suggest that many of the European Jews could return to their European countries of origin or immigrate to new lands. As for their children who might have been born in Palestine/Israel, they will have more claim to go back to their parents' European country of origin than the parents had a right to go to Palestine on the pretext of the 2,000 years ago argument.

On a different level, the question is raised as to the right of the Jews who were born in Palestine and Israel. It is said that these Jews have a right to be in Israel because they were born there. This argument is an appeal to a moral dictum: namely, a person should not be accountable for the deeds of others, including his parents. Assuming that the parents of the Israeli born Jews were intruders into Palestine, the person who was born in Palestine/Israel is not responsible for the deeds of his parents. This is a reasonable moral argument which has been advanced. There is, however, another moral argument which says that a person should not yield the benefits of someone else's aggression. As the parents of the boy or girl who was born in Palestine/Israel were aggressors, the child cannot enjoy the benefits of their intrusion.

The moral dilemma will be resolved if the young boys and girls who were born in Israel renounce their parents' act of intrusion into Palestine and beg of the Palestinian Arabs permission to stay. Then they would have all the rights to be a part of that society and the Arabs must then recognize their right as such. But the Israeli born Jews must first renounce their parents' act of intrusion as a basic prerequisite for being able to appeal to that moral rule.

With regard to the Peace Proposal, invariably the question is raised as to what will happen to the Jewish "state" when the Proposal is implemented.

We have suggested that the Proposal should be implemented over a period of twenty years. There are, of course, many questions left unanswered and we are really in no position to forsee exactly the details of the happenings twenty years hence. There are questions of Jewish owned land which is to be purchased by the Arabs, and the price of such land and property. There is the question of the gradual return of the Palestinian Arabs to their property and homes. There are problems of adjustment by the Jews as they return to their countries of origin or immigrate to lands of their choice, as well as problems of Palestinian Arabs as they return to their land. Many of these problems will have to be settled as they arise. Accordingly, we have suggested that there should be a United Nations High Commissioner to oversee and implement many detailed aspects and issues which will arise as the result of the implementation of the Peace Proposal.

As to what will happen to the "state" — as if the existence of the state is a sacred phenomenon — we wish to place the issue in its proper setting: The question is whether our concern should be with the human individual and his welfare or with the existence of a state.

If the individual Jew now in Israel might find his happiness, freedom, prosperity and security, say, in Vancouver, British Columbia, or in New York, as the majority of world Jews have found their freedom and security in these lands, and if the majority of the Jews now in Israel determine and decide to live amongst their kin and kith in other countries, then the question as to what will happen to the state will be a moot question indeed.

At any rate, what we forsee regarding the existence of the state is broadly something along this line: With European Jews leaving gradually and Christian and Moslem Palestinians gradually returning, the various parties would form what might become a joint Jewish-Christian-Moslem state. Such a state, as explained earlier, would be undemocratic by nature and definition. It is hoped that it would gradually change into a democratic society, ruled by the majority on the basis of political ideas and not on the ground of sectarian considerations. American liberals and civil libertarians should welcome such a development.

It has been said that the Peace Proposal is unrealistic. However, I have seen no "realistic" proposal offered by anyone and accepted by the parties involved. This at least is a new proposal — peaceful and humanitarian — and should be given the opportunity that it might be fulfilled. I suggest that the American Jews have the primary responsibility toward its fulfillment. They have been raising hundreds of millions of dollars every year to induce Jews from various parts of the world to go to Israel. I believe that if the American Zionist Jews want peace and are genuinely concerned with the welfare of their fellow Jews, they should raise money for *only one year* and offer it to all those Jews who are now in Israel, so that those who may wish to depart can do so. At least then we shall have the opportunity to know whether the Peace Proposal advanced here is a realistic one or otherwise.

I believe that our Peace Proposal is realistic. If the Zionist Jews disagree, let them try it!

V

Implementation

The Proposal advanced in the previous chapter may be as unattainable today as the proposal of Theodore Herzl was unattainable in its day. But if Herzl's proposal could be attained, even though it was damaging to the Jews, the Arabs, the West, and a threat to international peace, our Proposal, which looks toward the actual good of all parties concerned and toward international peace, should be implemented despite any and all difficulties.

Of course, a proposal has the prospects of being materialized as it receives the support and endorsement of the various parties who are interested in the general goals of that proposal.

Today, in the western world, there are many groups and organizations which have been interested in the improvement of relations with the Arab world and the Middle East. But these groups have been working invariably on cultural, religious, educational and philanthropic levels, and hardly on the political ground. These fields of activities are useful and valuable. However, in the long run, the question of peace is the paramount question and it is primarily a political issue as well as a humanitarian goal and the goal of humanity.

We believe that these organizations which have been directing their efforts toward so-called "cultural activities" should direct their energy, at least in part, to the question of peace in the

Middle East, and act on the political level.

Invariably, all Zionist Jewish organizations, whether they are cultural, religious, humanitarian, philanthropic or otherwise, have taken political stands and supported the general position of Israel. We believe that those organizations which are concerned with American and western interest and the welfare of the people of the Middle East should likewise take stands on the political level and not spend their time, energy, and money in the much-ado-about-nothing field of cultural activities.

To this end, we have called upon the American Friends of the Middle East to close its offices in the Arab world and bring its personnel back to the United States to work here on the political level. That will serve the general American-Arab cause far more than fifty offices that AFME might maintain in the Middle East.

There are many organizations concerned with humanitarian activities, and in terms of the Middle East, they work to help the one million, three hundred thousand Palestine Arab refugees. They try to provide the refugees with food, medicine, education and so on. These organizations could continue to feed the refugees for the next fifty years, and the problem will still be there as before. Hence, these organizations, too, should take stands on the political level, as they continue their humanitarian activities. Humanitarian activities by themselves are not fruitful if not backed by political activities.

Likewise, the various peace groups in America and Europe which are dedicated to the goal of peace and the welfare of the individual should take political stands on the problem of the Middle East even though that stand might be opposed by the Zionist Jews. Western liberal elements should recognize that

Zionism is a totalitarian movement of an intolerant group. To be in sympathy with victims of persecution is one thing; to support a vicious intolerant movement is another.

The liberal must recognize that to be *ipso facto* pro-Jewish is as prejudicial as to be *ipso facto* anti-Jewish. Likewise, it is as prejudicial to be pro-Negro, pro-Puerto Rican, pro-Indian, pro-Arab, etc. as to be against these groups. Hence, the liberals should not support all that a minority group does any more than the reactionaries should oppose minority group actions. In this particular connection, the liberals should not support Zionism just because it is the goal of some Jews, or even if it were the goal of all Jews. For Zionism is a reactionary movement and the Zionists are for freedom, equality, justice, peace and so on — only when these high goals serve the end of Jewish nationalism. In the era of "one world," Jewish nationalism is a violation of the spirit of the Age. Any organization dedicated to the cause of international peace cannot and should not cater to narrow nationism, Jewish or otherwise.

It is a fact that political organizations and political action represent the essence of the free society. The so-called "cultural" associations are permitted to function even in closed societies, whereas free political organizations are not. At any rate, to take a stand on behalf of peace is above politics and political action: it is an act compatible with the basic rules of the civil society and should receive the sanction and support of all religious, ethical and humanitarian groups.

In the West, and more specifically, in the United States of America, it is alarming that almost everyone concerned with peace and with the Middle East has been frightened by intolerant Zionists and forced to be silent on that issue. Everyone is afraid of political action and of taking any stand which might not appeal to the leaders of Zionism and Israel: People are afraid that unscrupulous Zionists would accuse them of anti-Semitism. Through this wicked device by which the Zionists equate anti-Zionism with anti-Semitism, Zionism has developed a most frightening weapon to silence the voices of opposition.

However, from the Zionists' narrow viewpoint, all the groups and organizations which are concerned with better understanding between America and the Arab world are considered pro-Arabs and anti-Jewish, even if such organizations are non-committal, non-political, impartial or neutral, or humanitarian. Once they are interested in the Arabs, from the viewpoint of Zionist totalitarianism, they are accused of being anti-Jewish and anti-Semites.

Accordingly, the leadership of these organizations such as AFME and the Near East Foundation and others, working as they do for cultural and humanitarian purposes, have an obligation to their members and to the principles of their organizations as well as the principles of the free society, to stand up and work on the political level as well. There is no reason why Jewish philanthropic organizations should support Israeli aggressions against the Arabs and to the detriment of America, and Christian organizations should not take stands in favor of peace and American interest in the Middle East. Likewise, Jewish cultural, humanitarian, and religious organizations have taken political stands in favor of Israel and against the United States. There is no reason why Christian and American cultural and humanitarian organizations should not take a stand in support of American interest and peace in the Middle East.

We have proposed that the gates of the United States, Canada, and other countries be opened for Israeli Jewish immigration to these lands. Under this Proposal, no one would force anyone to do anything. We are only calling for an opportunity for the free flow of people. Indeed, this is the most humanitarian attempt to provide the best of help and opportunity for the victims of Hitler. Ironically, Zionist Jewish leaders in America, who themselves preferred immigrating to the United States rather than going to Palestine and Israel, object to other victims of Hitlerism, who are now in Israel, to have the opportunity and the option to come to the United States. For whatever is good for the goose is, or should be, good for the gander. But Zionist Jewish leaders oppose and object to what will be for the actual good of their fellow Jews and in the interest of peace in the Middle East. Their behavior is one of double standards, unscrupulous, and exhibits clearly the similarity between the ends of Zionism and those of anti-Semitism.

Accordingly, I am requesting the endorsement of our Proposal by all groups concerned with better understanding between the West and the Arab world, and all organizations interested in peace. I am confident that these organizations are protected from any smear, for not even the Zionists could question their motives, integrity, humanitarianism, and the high goals of peace and human welfare which the Proposal advances.

There is, of course, nothing more frightening than the fear of fear itself. I am calling upon all freedom and peace-loving friends to emancipate themselves from the fear that the Zionists might somehow harm them. The Action Committee on American-Arab Relations has met the Zionists head-on: in the courts, in the legislative bodies, on the street, and on picket lines. No member of this organization has ever been harmed in the slightest in any way whatever, despite Zionists threats and the myth that they have the power to do this and that.

There are many individuals and groups who protest that they cannot take political stands on the ground that they "have not done this kind of thing before." This explanation should not be an excuse to keep a person within the old self-imposed shell. One should invariably look forward toward newer and more meaningful policies and programs. I invite all friends of better understanding between the West and the Arab world and all who are concerned with peace to emancipate themselves from the limitations of the past, and from whatever fear they might have, in order to adopt a new policy and join in endorsing and supporting the Proposal advanced here in the interest of peace in the Middle East. Those who permit the past to control the present will have no future.

I am also inviting the Jewish leaders, Zionist and otherwise, to support our Proposal for Peace, if their concern is indeed with peace and the good of their fellow Jews. Of course, the leaders of Jewish organizations, no less than the leaders of other organizations, having become members of the Establishment, are concerned invariably with their own position and power. Accordingly, there is a definite need to appeal to the Jewish community at large and to the rank and file, requesting them to examine the situation and question the position of their own leaders.

Indeed, the rank and file members of the Jewish community who have been asked again and again by their leaders to support Israel, financially as well as politically, are tired of those leaders. Furthermore, many individual Jews have expressed their general support and sympathy with the Proposal advanced in the previous pages. The fact is that many an American Jew would be very pleased and happy to invite his relatives to immigrate to America, much as the relatives would be very grateful and very happy to have the opportunity to thus immigrate. The members of Jewish communities everywhere should avail themselves of the right they have and the opportunity to provide the good life for their kin and kith by inviting those who wish to leave Israel to come to these lands.

There are two other groups to whom I should like to make a special appeal. One is to the Arab people and Arab governments. I believe that the Arab people and governments should overlook some of the injustices and insults directed against them by and through Zionism. They should somehow develop a greater sense of historic perspective and look forward to a gradual, peaceful evolution and solution of the problem over the next twenty years. Coupled with this, I believe that the Arabs should express their willingness to open their own gates at least for their former citizens, the Arab Jews, who left Arab lands and went to Israel. These former citizens should be given all the opportunities to return to their homes, and be given all civil and political rights, as Arab Moslems and Arab Christians enjoy.

Furthermore, the Arabs should provide compensation to the Jews who will be leaving Israel for the property the Jews own and leave behind. This, of course, should be arranged under a United Nations High Commissioner, who would take into consideration the gradual, and I stress *gradual*, return of the Palestinian Arab refugees to their homes, and the purchase and the compensation of the Jews for the land they had legally acquired and the improvements made thereupon. Also, the Arabs should accept as first class citizens any of the Jews who were born in Palestine and/or Israel, who would renounce their own parents' act of intrusion into Palestine and wish to become full partners of the new society.

Of course, the Arabs must publicize their cause to international and western audiences. However, they must recognize that they cannot present their case to western audiences through official information centers or consulates and embassies. Indeed, Zionist propaganda has been able to succeed, not because it was presented through the Israeli Information Center or the Israeli Embassy, but rather through local and private Jewish and Zionist sources and organizations. Hence, the Arabs should not expect too much from their own official informational activities as these offices are limited by their routines, the nature of their structures, and by many other considerations.

On the other hand, the Arabs who live in America and western societies and are citizens of these countries should recognize their own moral obligation to participate on the political level as free members of the free western societies. American Arabs should recognize that their efforts on an individual basis would be insignificant and almost useless and that only through organization and collective action can such efforts be meaningful. They should also recognize that organizations cannot function without financial support and assistance and that they should contribute generously toward such goals. It is the actual financial contributions, rather than *talking* about traditional Arab generosity, that are needed.

Then, I should like to make a special appeal to the Israelis: Please follow the good steps of the majority of world Jews who have employed common sense and enjoy a happy and creative life as members of the human race, among other members of the human race. I believe if I could make this appeal to the Israeli Jews directly, large segments of them will be willing to consider it and possibly heed the advice.

To this end, on 25 March 1966, I sent a telegram to the Israeli Ambassador to the United Nations, Mr. Michael S. Comay, requesting to meet with him so that he would provide for me the legal facilities to go to Israel and meet with the people to discuss the question of peace and the Proposal advanced here on behalf of peace. With hopes of meeting with the Israeli intellectuals at the Hebrew University and the man on the street, as well as the press and government officials, I had expected that this would be the beginning of the establishment of a people-to-people dialogue on behalf of peace.

Unfortunately, the Israeli Ambassador, being a member of the oligarchy and concerned with his post rather than with peace or the welfare of the individual Jews who are presently in Israel, failed to reply to my request. Surely, if he were genuinely interested in peace and the good of the people, he would have provided me with the opportunity to go to Israel, meet with the people, and discuss with them the Peace Proposal. I have no doubt that many of the people will examine the Proposal, heed its advice, and decide to depart in favor of the lands of opportunity and freedom in western Europe and North America. Undoubtedly, some of them would disregard the Proposal. But talking would hurt no one. At any rate, if the Israeli Jews should wish to depart, who is this Michael S. Comay of South Africa or Max Nussbaum of the United States to object to the express wishes and will of their co-religionists and fellow Jews who do not wish to stay in Israel? But oligarchies tend to perpetuate themselves in their own interest, and Michael Comay, as well as other leaders of Zionism and Israel, are no different. They have denied their own people an opportunity to exercise their own freedom and choose whether or not they wish to live in peace and amongst their relatives and friends. There are about three times as many Jews in America as in Israel, and if the Jews of Israel want to join their relatives and kin in America, they should not be denied the opportunity to do so. At least this opportunity should not be denied to the Jews of Israel by other Jews.

*   *   *

I am realistic enough to know that appeals are of no use, if concrete steps to implement the proposals are not taken. But one could not take concrete steps toward the implementation of the Proposal advanced here without funds. And the funds needed for the implementation of a gigantic peace project to which Zionism might be opposed must be large sums indeed.

I believe that to combat Zionist and Israeli leaders' opposition to bringing peace to the Middle East, one has to work in America even more than in the Middle East itself. For without Zionist pressure and influence in America and the West, Israel would not have been established. The need to combat Zionism and its opposition to peace, requires more than several hundred thousand dollars; it needs at least ten million dollars a year. In America, this amount should be provided from American sources.

The American oil companies, operating in the Arab world, have an annual net profit of more than one billion dollars. If these companies would contribute one thousandth of their profit, that would amount to one million dollars a year. Should they contribute 1% of the annual profit, it will amount to ten million dollars. *I believe that the American oil companies, with the huge profits they make out of their investment in the Arab world, have a moral obligation to contribute 1% of their profits in the interest of better American-Arab understanding, and in the interest of their own secure and perpetual investment in the Arab world.*

The American oil man is a courteous and friendly person, but he is so busy with hundreds of problems, and so engaged in the money-making business, that he seems to be absolutely unaware of the gravity of the situation in the Middle East, and of his responsibility to act on behalf of his own long range economic interest, as well as on behalf of the national interest of the United States. Many an oil executive has admitted the importance of political action and the need to employ political means on behalf of the mutual cause of American-Arab understanding. Yet, the same persons who are in a position to financially do something toward that end, invariably fail to do so. I have contacted the oil companies requesting them to participate actively in the mutual cause. While all of them have expressed interest and concern, most of them failed to participate. Many companies claimed that they had a policy not to engage in controversial issues; others stated openly that they feared Zionist intolerance and smear. Ironically, some of the richest of the companies pleaded lack of funds!

It is of course strange that companies with ties to Israel contribute hundreds of thousands of dollars for the evil end of Zionism and engage in controversial issues, while companies supposedly interested in the Arab world shy away from such participation.

The position of ARAMCO, one of the oldest established oil companies in the Arab world, which makes some four hundred million dollars every year, is most shameful. A few years ago, the president of ARAMCO, Mr. Thomas Barger, contributed on behalf of the company thirty-five thousand dollars to the 1,300,000 Arab refugees. Of course this was done after proper publicity and fanfare. At the same time, Elizabeth Taylor contributed one hundred thousand dollars to some Zionist project. By comparison to Miss Taylor's contribution, the oil company's contribution to the cause of American-Arab understanding was shamefully meager and inadequate indeed. ARAMCO's president states that his company has a policy not to interfere in political activities. Of course, ARAMCO should not interfere in the political life of Saudi Arabia. But in America, it should discharge its duties and responsibilities as other companies and firms do.

But while ARAMCO has presented an unacceptable excuse, one Mr. Howard Page of Standard Oil of New Jersey, has not even had the courtesy to reply to the several letters which I have written to him on behalf of the mutual American-Arab cause. I received a prompt reply from Mr. Page once, when I mentioned a smearing article which had appeared in *The Nation.* He replied promptly, disclaiming any ties to that article. However, when I requested him again to contribute financially to the mutual cause, he failed to even acknowledge receipt of my letter. As a matter of fact, I do not know whether Mr. Page is dead or alive, even though I would not be astonished if I ran into him in one of the very many Arab parties in New York, Washington and elsewhere. There are many such individuals whose concern and interest in the Arabs is to attend Arab functions and parties and of course the gullible Arabs invite such parasites again and again in the name of Arab hospitality. The Standard Oil Company of New Jersey makes some 300 million dollars a year, yet its officials do not contribute a penny to the mutual cause of better American-Arab understanding.

To repeat, I believe that there is a need for at least ten million dollars a year to perpetuate the ideas, and finally to bring about the implementation of, the Peace Proposal. The American oil companies operating in the Arab world have the moral obligation to provide the ten million dollars annually.

It should be abundantly clear, and I should like to state it in the simplest language possible, that by Jehovah, by God, and by Allah, *the oil fields in the Arab world will be nationalized unless American policy toward the question of Palestine is changed.* Many an oil executive is convinced of this fact, yet either greed or utter thoughtlessness, or a complete lack of appreciation of his rights as an American citizen and his duties as a free person in a free society, or his timidity, or all these factors combined have made these oil men incapacitated and unable to stand on their own two feet to defend their own long range material interest, the moral and political interests of the United States, and the future of American-Arab understanding. Ironically, and except for their evil end, the Zionist Jews who exercise their rights are better citizens than the timid souls who do not appreciate their position as Americans with rights and obligations.

The Arabs cannot depend on the American oil men. The American oil man is not concerned with the welfare of the Arabs; he is not even concerned seriously with America and its future. What American oil men and other "friends" of the Arabs do is to contribute little bits here and there for "charitable purposes," "educational institutions," and "refugee relief." But let it be made absolutely clear that while these contributions may be of some temporary use, in the long run they are useless if not harmful! Such little contributions might relieve some of the sense of guilt that these friends might have and might meet some of their sense of moral responsibility and obligation. But it would be more a case of the ostrich trying to avoid the inevitable by looking elsewhere or not looking at all. I am afraid that the position of the American oil companies and other so-called friends who are afraid of Zionism is like that of the ostrich indeed. For whenever the ostrich is frightened, it assumes a position which is both vulgar and vulnerable. These friends and companies should emancipate themselves from that fear and assume their normal posture as free persons in a free society.

Many years ago, a pamphleteer wrote certain passages which are pertinent today. In his AMERICAN CRISIS I, Tom Paine urged the American people to rise to the occasion. This was written while Paine was accompanying Washington's forces during the retreat in New Jersey, and the Revolution seemed to be at its lowest ebb. Paine called upon the people to stand up and be counted:

> These are the times that try men's souls . . . . The summer soldier and sunshine patriot will, in this crisis, shrink from the service of his country; but he that stands it now, deserves the love and thanks of men and women. Tyranny, like hell, is not easily conquered; yet we have this consolation with us, that the harder the conflict, the more glorious

the triumph.

I am inviting the knowledgeable, the businessmen, the liberals, the humanists, the conservatives, the peace groups, and all who are concerned with a better world for tomorrow, to stand up and face the crisis of today.

The present crisis in the Middle East and the dangerous situation there which may lead to a global conflict is the result of the disease of anti-Semitism and the manipulation of that plague by the Zionists, who threaten and terrify the innocent even more than the guilty. This wicked manipulation of the western sense of guilt by the Zionists has given them a weapon as powerful as those employed by the totalitarian regimes. And it must be admitted that Zionist totalitarianism, like hell, is not easily conquered. But, as these also are times which try men's souls, we must be ready to meet the test, and try to conquer that tyranny.

I have invited the support and endorsement of our Peace Proposal by friends of American-Arab understanding and by all concerned with peace. I have no doubt that while there will be many difficulties and some temporary setbacks, and there will be those who might shy away sheepishly, frightened of Zionism and shrink from their responsibility — I have no doubt that in the long run

We Will Win.

Epilogue

During November and December of 1966, I visited the Arab world for the first time in seventeen years. I visited Beirut, Kuwait, Bahrain, Riyadh, Amman, Jerusalem, Baghdad, and Cairo. I met with Arab kings and heads of state, Foreign Ministers, and Prime Ministers. I met with members of the press, Arab intellectuals, and the man on the street.

More important, I met with the Palestinian Arabs, their leaders and rank and file, their poets, their intellectuals, young and old. I saw the Palestinians in Kuwait, in Bahrain, in Riyadh, and everywhere else. I visited the refugee camps in Jericho and in and around Jerusalem and Bethlehem. I visited Qalqilia and Tolkaram, where the rich Arab soil across the imaginary demarcation line has been taken over by Polish and Hungarian Jewish immigrants and denied to the Christian and Moslem Arab owners.

And I visited Beit Safafa where the demarcation line cuts the center of the main street of this Arab village, dividing families into two "nationalities" legally at war with one another! When there is a marriage in the divided Arab village, members of the family from both sides of the "iron curtain" go to the dividing fence to extend greetings and congratulations. Likewise when there is a death in the village, the villagers go to the dividing fence with the coffin to mourn their beloved. This demonstrates all too vividly the most tragic result of Zionist intrusion into Palestine — when a family must be divided even in the presence of death, the only peace these tormented people ever attain.

Epilogue

It is redundant but necessary to report that the Arabs generally and the Palestinians particularly were unanimous that they have no alternative but to regain their homes in Palestine. This feeling and determination of the people of Palestine to regain their land receives the backing of millions of Moslems and Christians. It would also receive the backing of the Jews in the West, if they only knew the nature of the conflict and the terrible tragedy which has befallen the Palestinians.

In the Middle East, I discussed the Peace Proposal of the Action Committee on American-Arab Relations with Arab high government officials, as well as with the Arab press, and Arab intellectuals and the man on the street. Our general position, to be restated, calls for opportunities to be provided for the Israeli Jews to return either to their countries of origin or to immigrate to countries of their choice. Furthermore, it calls upon the Arabs to provide prompt and adequate compensation to the Jews for the property they own and leave behind. It maintains that all the Jews who may wish to stay in the Holy Land for purely religious purposes should stay there, and it calls upon the Arabs to take back their former citizens, the Arab Jews, and accord them their legal and political rights. And finally, the Proposal contemplates a gradual achievement of the goal of restoring peace to the Holy Land over a period of twenty years.

The Arabs were generally sympathetic with the general goals of the Proposal. They were unanimously committed to the proposition that the question of Palestine should be resolved peacefully, and that opportunities should be provided for the European Jews to return either to their countries of origin in western Europe or to lands of greater opportunities in North America and elsewhere.

However, the various Arab leaders as well as Arab intellectuals and the man on the street held some reservations regarding three aspects of the Proposal.

First, with regard to our suggestion that the Arabs should offer compensation to the Jews for the property they own and leave behind. The Arabs stated that the Jews had taken over much of the Arab land, and they had used that Arab land, enjoying the benefits and profits it yielded for them. Furthermore, the creation of Israel had diverted much of Arab energy and capital toward investment in nonproductive fields and had thereby damaged Arab economy for a long period of time. Accordingly, the Arabs felt that it would be rather unfair and unjust if they had to pay compensation to the Jews for the property the Jews "own." This property does not exceed 6½% of the land of Palestine, a fact which has been confirmed by the United Nations.[17]

I stated that the Israelis had made a great deal of improvement over that 6½% of the land, and at least this improvement, which had increased the value of the land, should be taken into consideration, and at any rate, the Arabs should undertake to provide compensation as part of their obligation toward a peaceful settlement of the problem.

Secondly, the Arabs had reservations regarding the return of their former citizens, the Arab Jews, to the Arab countries. They felt that these Arab Jews had renounced their Arab citizenship after several hundred or thousand years during which they were part and parcel of the Arab society. They said, for example, that the Jews of Iraq had lived there for more than two thousand years, yet they (the Jews) maintained that, despite the two thousand years, they were foreigners in Iraq, and that their home was in the far away enemy State of Israel. Of course, Israel being an enemy of the Arab people of Iraq, any such Iraqi Jew claiming loyalty and attachment to the enemy was indeed a traitor to Iraq, as is anyone who gives aid and comfort to an enemy of the state. The Arabs felt that to permit such once-traitors, or at least persons who had at best a double loyalty, to return to Iraq, might be a dangerous undertaking for the safety of the state.

I argued that Jews who left Egypt, Algeria, Iraq, and Morocco, might have done so under pressure of the Zionists and by their instigation, and due to a misunderstanding of the nature of the problem. At any rate, I felt that they should be given another opportunity and be given their full rights and the property they owned before their renunciation of their citizenship, and that the Arabs should do so as part of the peaceful settlement of the problem of Palestine. Surely the Arabs could not expect the European Jews to go back to Europe or immigrate to North America without permitting the Arab Jews to return to the Arab countries.

Finally, the Arabs had some reservations regarding the length of time we had proposed for the peaceful settlement of the problem. They felt that a period of twenty years was much too long. It was the life time of a generation, and it would be unfair to expect the Arabs to wait twenty more long years for the settlement of a problem in which they were only the parties by default. The problem was the atrocities of an insane European committed against the European Jews, and there was no reason why the Arabs should suffer because of the insane behavior of a European.

I recalled a discussion between a Zionist and a Palestinian

Arab in which the Zionist suggested that after eighteen years of one generation of Palestinians having been away, it is only a "matter of time" for the generation of Palestine refugees to die out and the ties of the Palestinians to the land of Palestine to be dissolved. The Palestine Arab stated that indeed it was a "matter of time" and that this matter of time would take at least 4,000 years. Surely, he suggested, if the Jews had not forgotten Palestine after 2,000 years, and they came from Poland, Russia, and elsewhere, it will take the Palestinians at least 4,000 years to dissolve their ties to Palestine. I said that if this is the measure of Palestine Arab determination to eventually regain their land even after 4,000 years, then surely the matter of twenty years should be a simple one, and that the Palestinians should become more patient and therefore be more disposed toward the solution of the problem peacefully, within twenty years, in accordance with the Peace Proposal of the Action Committee on American-Arab Relations.

* * *

On 3 February 1967, a delegation from the Action Committee on American-Arab Relations met with Arthur J. Goldberg, United States Ambassador to the United Nations. Ambassador Goldberg had met earlier with the leaders of the American Jewish community. This meeting with the leaders of the American Arabs represented a recognition of the significance of the American Arabs as part of the American political scene. This was an historic occasion, for I believe it is of utmost importance for the American Arabs and the friends of the American-Arab cause to participate on the political level on questions concerning the Middle East and American policy toward that region.

Such participation on the political level will bring about a balance in the situation which under the pressure of the Zionist Jews and the politicians seeking the so-called "Jewish vote" has become imbalanced to the detriment of all concerned.

The delegation presented to Goldberg a five point program and the Peace Proposal of the organization, stressing the question of peace in the Middle East. Later, the delegation met with representatives of the American and international press and news agencies and announced a three-year ten million dollar plan to aid the emigrating Israelis.

At the meeting with Ambassador Goldberg, the delegation requested the Ambassador to prevail upon the Johnson Administration and the American government to amend and change the United States immigration laws with the view of providing legal facilities for the Israeli Jews who might wish to immigrate to the United States. It was suggested that if the United States takes the initiative in this field, Canada, Australia, as well as western European and other countries might follow the American move and leadership.

The three-year ten million dollar plan was to provide the actual financial opportunity for those Israelis who may wish to leave. The American Arab delegation invited the United Jewish Appeal and other humanitarian Jewish organizations to participate and cooperate with the Action Committee and match the ten million dollars. The new proposed fund would aid the emigrating Israelis and thus would be in the interest of the human individual Jews and in the interest of peace in the Middle East.

The American Arabs are extending their hand in friendship and say "Shalom." It is the earnest hope of all peace-loving people to see the American Jews cooperate with the American Arabs in the interest of the individual Jews as well as international peace.

Appendix

In our endeavors to combat anti-Semitism and anti-Gentile-ism we have written to many prominent individuals and organizations, asking them to support our program of study at Columbia University on the question of "Jewish Beliefs and Anti-Gentile-ism," much as the University of California had studied "Christian Beliefs and Anti-Semitism."

The response to our appeal was gratifying. Those who were indeed opposed to prejudice from any source, Christian or Jewish, wrote condemning anti-Semitism and anti-Gentile-ism. These were gratifying replies from courageous men, who were ready to call a spade a spade. I am describing these independent minded men of good will as "courageous" because of the terrible circumstances in which we live, and during which Zionist totalitarianism is employing the power of blackmail and smear, accusing whomever might disagree with Zionism and might find some fault with some Jews, of being anti-Semites.

These men who oppose anti-Semitism and supported a thorough and objective examination of the question of anti-Gentile-ism by a university of high repute such as Columbia, are courageous because they stood against the general trend.

I am reproducing in the following pages some of the replies we received. However, a word or two about some of them is necessary. We had requested the Anti-Defamation League to join with us and co-sponsor the project at Columbia, on the ground that the Anti-Defamation League was genuinely interested in the elimination of prejudice from all sources. It is with much regret that we have to report that the Anti-Defamation League refused to cooperate with us, and we charge that the League seems to be more concerned with picking on the Christians and exposing Christian prejudice toward the Jews, and not about Jewish prejudice toward the Christians.

The Anti-Defamation League failed to cooperate with us on the study of Jewish beliefs and anti-Gentile-ism, apparently on the ground that it believes that "the Jews can do no wrong." This is the other side of the coin, used by anti-Semites, on which it is written that "the Jews can do no right." I had also written to Charles Glock and Rodney Stark, who had conducted the study of Christian Beliefs and Anti-Semitism at the University of California. I requested them to advise me whether they had taken into consideration the question of anti-Gentile-ism as a factor in creating anti-Semitism. These scholars failed to reply, evidently ashamed of themselves as they recognized that their "scholarly" effort was based on a one-sided assumption.

On the other hand, the highly renowned Yeshiva University wrote in the best tradition of scholars and humanists. It said that the University was "alert to the need to eliminate Jewish prejudices against the Christians and/or Gentiles." However, the University felt that it could not subscribe to the idea that because the concept of the "chosen people" was misunderstood, one should eliminate it any more than one would want to abolish sex because people practice sodomy. Moreover, the University stated that Jewish prejudice against the Christians and/or Gentiles has not been as destructive in human history as its counterpart.

While I agree fully that Jewish prejudice against the Gentiles has not been as destructive as its counterpart, I do not believe that the analogy between the misunderstanding of the concept of the "chosen people" and the misusing of sex is a valid one. The concept of "chosen people" is a myth created by people, and circulated amongst them, whereas sex is the most essential natural function of human existence. And so, while we can discard myths, particularly those which have proven to be dangerous and useless, we cannot discard sex, even if sex were misused.

Also, I should like to mention the fact that, despite repeated efforts to reach the National Conference of Christians and Jews, asking for their cooperation and their view on the question of anti-Semitism and anti-Gentile-ism, we received no reply. Likewise, Francis Cardinal Spellman failed to respond to our repeated attempts to learn his position on the matter. Whether the National Conference of Christians and Jews and Cardinal Spellman believe that the Jews, or at least some Jews, have no prejudice toward the Christian, I do not know. I do know, however, that to me, a Cardinal is as good as an ordinary person only if he performs his function. By failing to reply, Cardinal Spellman was discourteous as well as negligent in performing his duties.

I have no doubt that many of those who go overboard in trying to protect and befriend the Jews, or defend and befriend any minority group too much, may be at heart prejudiced against that group, yet they sugar-coat their prejudice by going overboard in the opposite direction. This may indeed be the case with the Cardinal as well as with the Christian members of the National Conference of Christians and Jews.

But we are all grateful to the courageous organizations and individuals who opposed anti-Semitism and anti-Gentile-ism. Their response would revitalize our faith in the open society. Furthermore, their stand is a contribution to peace. For the opposition to anti-Semitism and anti-Gentile-ism is a step toward the ultimate elimination of these diseases, and is an essential condition for peace in the Middle East.

A special word of gratitude is due to the National Council of Churches, to Richard Cardinal Cushing, to the Right Reverend (Retired) Bishop of California James A. Pike, to President Thomas B. MacDormand of the Eastern Baptist Theological Seminary, as well as to Professors David Riesman, Hannah Arendt, Paul A. Reynolds, and many others who wrote expressing their opposition to anti-Semitism and anti-Gentile-ism and contributed to my own better understanding of the issues involved.

national council of the churches of christ in the u.s.a.

475 RIVERSIDE DRIVE, NEW YORK, N. Y. 10027   telephone: 870-2141

bishop reuben h. mueller, president   r. h. edwin espy, general secretary

September 16, 1966

Dr. M. T. Mehdi, Secretary-General
The Action Committee on American-Arab Relations
441 Lexington Avenue
New York, N. Y. 10017

Dear Dr. Mehdi:

We in the National Council of Churches of course are opposed to anti-Semitism and anti-Gentile-ism, and consequently I want to repeat the observation I made in my letter of August 10 -- that this subject is an important one.

However, inasmuch as the National Council was not involved in the University of California study of "Christian Belief and Anti-Semitism," it seems to me best and right that we not involve ourselves in the study of "anti-Gentile-ism" that you have proposed.

Thank you for sharing this interesting information with us.

Sincerely yours,

Reuben H. Mueller

cc: Dr. R. H. Edwin Espy

YESHIVA UNIVERSITY

AMSTERDAM AVENUE AND 186th STREET
NEW YORK 33, N. Y.   •   LOrraine 8-8400

ASSISTANT TO THE PRESIDENT

June 20, 1966

Dr. M. T. Mehdi
Secretary-General'
The Action Committee on
 American-Arab Relations
441 Lexington Avenue
New York, New York

Dear Dr. Mehdi:

Your letter to Dr. Samuel Belkin of Yeshiva University was
referred to me for reply.

Certainly our entire faculty is alert to the need to eliminate
Jewish prejudices against Christians and/or Gentiles. We
are as anxious to eliminate religious prejudices as racial
prejudices. Many members of our faculty deal with this
problem. By the same token, however, we cannot subscribe
to the idea that because the concept of the "chosen people" is
misunderstood we should eliminate it any more than we would
want to abolish sex because people practice sodomy. Moreover, we do not feel that Jewish prejudice against Christians
and/or Gentiles has been as destructive in human history as its
counterpart; nor can it be in the foreseeable future. We are
concerned to eliminate the prejudices because it does not
ennoble and is unworthy of our religious commitment and
our belief in a God who created man in his image. But we do
not visualize any clear and present danger emerging from it.

Very cordially yours,

Emanuel Rackman
Assistant to the President

Center for the Study of Democratic Institutions
THE FUND FOR THE REPUBLIC, INC.
Box 4068, Santa Barbara, California 93103

August 19, 1966

Dr. M. T. Mehdi
Secretary-General
The Action Committee on American-
   Arab Relations
P. O. Box 416
New York, N. Y. 10017

My dear Dr. Mehdi:

Thank you for sharing with me information
as to the proposed study on "Jewish Belief and
Anti-Gentile-ism." As one who has found valuable the
Glock and Stark study, I would find most useful the
fruits of the study which you propose. I would be
personally interested and it would also be helpful
in connection with my work at the Center for the Study
of Democratic Institutions.

I certainly do hope that it goes forward and
would appreciate further information as the plan
develops.

With every good wish,

Sincerely yours,

James A. Pike

The Rt. Rev. James A. Pike

New York office:
136 East 57 Street
New York, N.Y. 10022
(212) 753-1340

The Eastern Baptist Theological Seminary
PHILADELPHIA, PA. 19151
Eastern Baptist College
ST. DAVIDS, PA.

PRESIDENT THOMAS B. McDORMAND
B.D., Th.D., D.D., LL.D.
CITY LINE AND LANCASTER AVENUE
PHILADELPHIA, PA. 19151

June 20, 1966

Dr. M. T. Mehdi
P. O. Box 416
New York, New York 10017

Dear Dr. Mehdi:

I concur in the wisdom of your letter of recent date suggesting the necessity of an effort to dissuade Jews from any type of anti-
Gentile propoganda or action.

You are perfectly right that all concerns of
goodwill involve "two-way streets", and that
there has been a tendency and is a tendency,
no doubt, on the part of extreme Jewry to
look with suspicion or hostility upon non-
Jews in general.   To the extent that this
may be true, there is an opportunity for men
of goodwill to band themselves together in
an effort to uproot any such attitude or
tendency anywhere in the world.

Yours sincerely,

Thomas B. McDormand
President

TBM:inc

Minnesota COUNCIL OF CHURCHES

122 West Franklin Avenue, Minneapolis, Minnesota, 55404   Telephone 332-2571

OFFICERS

Rev. Robert A. Caine
President

Dr. Floyd Massey, Jr.
Rev. Donald W. Schmidt
Mrs. Walter F. Mueller
Vice Presidents

Andrew W. Hobart
Treasurer

Mrs. Arthur O. Hoistad
Recording Secretary

STAFF

Rev. Alton M. Motter
Executive Director

Rev. George K. Tjaden
Director, Department of Town
and Country Church Life

Alice I. Huston
Director, Department of
Christian Education

Rev. Willis J. Merriman
Director, Departments of
Christian Social Relations
and Pastoral Services

Mrs. John D. Hale
Audio-Visual Librarian

Dr. Hayden L. Stright
Executive Secretary Emeritus

Harold W. Jenkins
Director of Finance,
Minnesota Protestant
Center

Mrs. Harold W. Ruopp
Personal Counselor

Rev. Raymond G. Baines
Executive Director
United Church Committee
on Indian Work

Bruce Sifford
Director, Minnesota
Church Committee
On Radio and TV

June 14, 1966

Dr. M. T. Mehdi
Secretary - General
Action Committee on American-Arab Relations
441 Lexington Avenue
New York, New York 10017

Dear Dr. Mehdi:

I read your letter concerning a possible study on Jewish
belief and Anti-Gentilism with much interest. Such a study
would contribute much to some of the underlying causes of
Anti-Semitism and should be extremely helpful to Jews as
well as Gentiles. I have just conducted a radio discussion
on the book Christian Beliefs and Anti-Semitism and I am
convinced that a study such as your purpose would help to
round out this entire subject. That could make a constructive contribution toward establishing better relationships
with the great segments of the people of the world. I
trust that it may become a reality.

Sincerely,

Alton M. Motter
Executive Director

AMM:ia

ANTI-DEFAMATION LEAGUE
Of B'nai B'rith
315 LEXINGTON AVENUE, NEW YORK, N. Y. 10016, MUrray Hill 9-7400

June 14, 1966

Dr. M. T. Mehdi
The Action Committee on American-Arab Relations
P. O. Box 146
New York, New York 10017

Dear Dr. Mehdi:

In response to your June 8th letter, be advised

that the Anti-Defamation League is not at all interested

in any cooperative effort with you or your organization.

Very truly yours,

AF:hmg   Arnold Forster

"...Dedicated to translating democratic ideals into a way of life for all Americans in our time."

CARDINAL'S RESIDENCE
2101 COMMONWEALTH AVENUE
BRIGHTON, MASSACHUSETTS 02135

August 13, 1966

Dear Doctor Mehdi:

Thank you for your letter of August the 8th.

With regard to anti-Semitism and anti-Gentile-ism, I am opposed to both of them and with equal vigor. I am sorry, however, I cannot lend any financial support to this project because I am overwhelmed with pledges, promises and commitments amounting to millions of dollars here at home and in Latin America where I have over one hundred priests, and to causes in other parts of the world.

I have been "out of circulation" for the past two and a half months due to serious illness and as a result I am far, far behind in my work as a beggar for Christ for all worthy causes.

With all good wishes, I am

Yours most cordially,

Richard Cardinal Cushing
Archbishop of Boston

Dr M. T. Mehdi
P.O. Box 416
New York, N.Y. 10017

Footnotes

1. M. T. Mehdi, A NATION OF LIONS . . . CHAINED (New World Press, San Francisco & New York) 1962, pp. 62 ff.

2. It is estimated that there are today some fifteen million Jews in the world. About two million of them are in Israel, which represents some 12%. Thirteen million, which represents more than 88%, have declined the opportunity to go "home."

3. J. Robert Moskin, "Prejudice in Israel," LOOK MAGAZINE, 5 October 1965.

4. ABINGTON SCHOOL DISTRICT vs. SCHAMPP, (1963) 374 US 222.

5. For the complete story of this case and the above quotations, see THE NEW YORK TIMES, 19 February 1967, 21 February 1967, 24 February 1967, 26 February 1967.

6. Charles Glock and Rodney Stark, CHRISTIAN BELIEFS AND ANTI-SEMITISM, p. 205.

7. There are some who doubt that Jews might have prejudice toward others. There is no doubt that most Jews are prejudiced at least toward the Arabs. The word "prejudice," as it is commonly used within the scope of race relations, refers to a sort of instantaneous feeling and/or conviction that some individual, because of his group identity, is bad, evil, a wrongdoer, or otherwise obnoxious.

For example, when the word "Jew" is mentioned to an anti-Semite, he becomes at once unconsciously ill-at-ease, irritable, and unhappy, and he might express his feelings with a little cry, "Oh, God, no!" The word "Arab" would evoke the same kind of feeling in the heart of many a Jew.

Of course, the Arabs today are also prejudiced toward the Jews, because they are so emotionally involved in the struggle against Zionism, that they fail to differentiate between Jews and Zionists. To the majority of the Arabs, the American Jews are as bad as the

Germans are considered by the Jews. The same kind of feeling that the word "German" would evoke in the majority of world Jewry would be evoked in the heart of every Arab at the sound of the word, "Jew," even though historically the Arab and Moslem attitudes toward the Jews and others was not a prejudicial one.

I believe that Arab intellectuals should educate the Arab masses as to the exact nature of the conflict in Palestine between political Zionism and Arab nationalism and make the clear cut distinction between Jews and Judaism on the one hand, and Zionism on the other hand. The Arabs should make the distinction between Judaism and Zionism even if the Zionists attempt to confuse the issue by identifying one with the other.

8. While on the one hand the conflict between these two Jewish and Christian claims to the status of chosen people might be at the root of the problem of prejudice in the West, on the other hand, it has been said that the western and American civilization is based on a Judeo-Christian or a Hebraic-Greco foundation. This, at best, is only part of the story. For a fuller explanation of the foundation of modern western civilization, one would have to go to a wider area: the foundation of American society is set on a Judeo-Christian-Islamic or Hebraic-Greco-Arabic base. This is not a chauvinistic or ethnocentric claim. However, if the suggestion sounds strange, let us remember that if it were not for the Arabic numerals, Islamic philosophy, the Arab contributions to science and invention of instruments of navigation, America might not have been discovered and the present standing of western civilization would not be as high.

Even more startling, and more interesting is to observe that the American civilization is not as much Judaic and Christian as it is "Islamic" in its orientation and spirit. The American society of today does not believe in the primitive Hebraic concept of retribution of an eye for an eye as a device to maintain the social order and administer justice. Nor does it subscribe to the highly idealistic Christian concept of utter forgiveness as evidenced in calling upon the faithful to turn the other cheek and the Commandment, "Thou shalt not kill." On the contrary, and in the best tradition of Islam, America believes in retribution and forgiveness at the same time. This is not because the American society has known and appreciated Islam, but because the pragmatic needs of human society evolve on the model of any middle of the road philosophy such as Islam and its spirit of rational idealism.

The question of sanction is the foundation of every society. Islam does not believe in the eye for an eye principle, nor does it advocate the principle of turning the other cheek and thou shalt not kill. On the contrary, it believes that on occasions, sanctions should be provided to punish the wrongdoer and prevent him from further acts of violence, but then it also recommends that it is better to forgive. However, forgiveness here must come only after the ability of the injured party to apply sanction is clearly established. It is only then that his forgiving will be meritorious as he does indeed rise above the legitimate right. In this way, Islam is the middle of the road and the happy compromise between Judaism and Christianity in an attempt to combine absolute rationalism with absolute idealism.

The American society of today also believes, as it should, in the application of sanctions against the violators of the law, but then there are many kinds of mitigating circumstances which bring about a mixture of sanction, rehabilitation, and forgiveness.

While comparing America and the worlds of Islam and the Arabs, it is interesting to note that the Jews have been at the heights of their creative ability in America of today and during the period of Arabic-Islamic civilization. For the spirit of Islamic liberalism provided that atmosphere which is needed for creative work, scientific inquiry, and speculative thinking. Jewish philosophical and scientific contributions were possible only because of the existence of that kind of environment. The environment of freedom in America today is likewise providing the opportunity for the Jews, as well as for all other individuals, or groups, to be creative in the arts and sciences.

The late Sir Victor Gollancz described himself as a "liberal Judeo-Christian." I believe that had he been exposed to the rational idealism of Islam, as I have been fortunate enough to be exposed, he would have described himself as a "Judeo-Christian-Moslem," as I do. Indeed we are all, particularly those who are not dogmatic adherents of organized religious doctrines, act and behave, knowingly or unwittingly, in this spirit, regardless of how we might describe ourselves.

9. The conflict between church and state does not exist in Islam, whereas it has been part and parcel of western history. The reason is that when Christianity came to Rome, the Roman state was fully established, and it had already claimed full authority and demanded the full loyalty of man. The new religious authority also claimed full power and demanded complete loyalty. Hence, there was the

conflict between church and state, which ultimately was replaced by the concept of separation of church and state as a means to accommodate the two claims. The situation in Islam is different, for when Islam was proclaimed in Arabia, there was no "state" and the new religion became the foundation of both temporal as well as spiritual authority.

10. We must distinguish between this general trend toward the triumph of the individual and universalism in the West on the one hand, and the rise of nationalism in Asia and Africa on the other.

The rise of modern nationalism in Asia and Africa is a necessary step toward gradual development of constitutionalism and ultimate democratization. The West did go through this stage of development and it is now moving away from nationalism toward universalism. Hence, the advent of Zionist nationalism at this stage of progress in the West is a movement contrary to the general trend toward universalism, and so, deplorable even if the advent of nationalism in Asia and Africa, seen in its historic perspective, could be considered a step forward. Of course, nationalism in Asia and Africa, after attaining its immediate goals of liberation and unification will have to give in to democratization, the triumph of the individual and universalism. Only in that sense, could nationalism of Asia and Africa be justified temporarily and temporarily condoned.

11. It is a historical fact that Islam has less prejudice toward other religious groups and its pride is in its "liberalism and tolerance." Nevertheless, the Moslems of the twentieth century should be willing to submit the teachings of Islam to a scholarly examination and if it is found that there are elements in Islam which might lead to prejudice toward other peoples, these elements should be removed or reinterpreted in new terms, with the view of eliminating prejudice.

12. JEWISH ENCYCLOPEDIA, Volume VII, p. 541.

13. Dagobert D. Runes, CONCISE DICTIONARY OF JUDAISM (Philosophical Library, New York) 1959, p. 217.

14. JEWISH ENCYCLOPEDIA, Volume VII, p. 541.

15. The Talmud is considered by one Jewish scholar to be one of the world's ten great works of divinely inspired literature. There are many references in the Talmud which stimulate prejudice toward non-

Jews. In parts 22a and 48a of the Tractite Abodah Zarah — and in many other sections too numerous to note here for our purposes — there are indications amounting to evidence that when heathens and/or idolators are mentioned, these terms actually refer to all non-Jews, and in certain cases they especially refer to Christians. The following, taken from part 22b of Abodah Zarah, is indicative of the contemptuous attitude of the Talmud toward the non-Jews: ". . . neither should we buy male cattle from heathen women, for fear of their having used them for immoral practice! . . . — Why should we not leave female animals alone with female heathens? — . . . because heathens frequent their neighbor's wives, and should one by chance not find her in, and find the cattle there, he might use it immorally. You may also say that even if he should find her in he might use the animal, as a master has said: Heathens prefer the cattle of the Israelites to their own wives . . ."

16. In March 1967, Mr. David Ben-Gurion visited the United States of America for three weeks. His main purpose was to encourage American Jews to immigrate to Israel and settle in the Negev. Ben-Gurion admitted on many occasions that Israel has no future except if the Negev is to be settled and that only American Jews can make that future secure by leaving America to settle in the Negev.

The New York Times reported that Ben-Gurion wanted the Jewish "elite" from America to settle in Israel. Those Jews who felt the "obligation" to go to Israel were the elite of the American Jews. In the nationwide television program, "Meet The Press," Mr. Ben-Gurion said that those Jews who do not go to Israel are not Jews.

The irony, of course, was that the American Jews were able to stomach these continued insults upon their loyalty to America and their identity as Jews.

The Action Committee on American-Arab Relations sent a "truth squad" to follow Ben-Gurion to Miami, Philadelphia, Los Angeles, Chicago, New York and Boston in order to bring the real Ben-Gurion to the fore. And the real Ben-Gurion was a dangerous man: He was dangerous to the American Jewish community, which he wanted to uproot, and he was a threat to peace in the Middle East, for the more Jews who go to that area, the greater the danger and threat to peace.

In his attempt to get the American Jews out of America, Mr. Ben-Gurion was working along the same general lines and toward the same goals as every anti-Semite from George Lincoln Rockwell to

Gerald L. K. Smith. Both Ben-Gurion and the anti-Semites want the American Jews out of America. They might have two different reasons, but they are working toward the same disruptive, disturbing and evil end.

Mr. Ben-Gurion was billed by his press agent as the "co-founder" of Israel. The "other" co-founder, or indeed the real founder and the father of Israel is of course Hitler, and Mr. Ben-Gurion might be considered the midwife. For, as stated earlier, if there had been no Hitler and no anti-Semitism, Zionism would not have been able to succeed in uprooting European Jews in order to settle them in Palestine. And Ben-Gurion, obsessed as he is with the creation of a viable state, and knowing full well that Hitler was the real father of Israel and that the present-day Israel is not a viable state, and it will become viable only if American Jews go there — Ben-Gurion, knowing these, is obsessed enough and unscrupulous enough to want to see anti-Semitism and prejudice stirred up against American Jews if that is the means of getting American Jews out of America. Not that Ben-Gurion wants the rise of another Hitler in America. But he would welcome a measure of prejudice and anti-Semitism to prevent what he has described as "the danger of assimilation of American Jews in the mainstream of American life." And also, to make the Jews ever-ready to leave America and settle in Israel.

From the viewpoint of a man obsessed with the idea of creating a viable state, it is understandable if he goes to any length in the interest of fulfilling his goal. Indeed, Ben-Gurion did his best to create prejudice against American Jews. This was done in a very subtle and highly sophisticated way. Ben-Gurion was able to raise in the American mind the question as to whether the American Jews are a permanent part of the American society or whether they are here on a temporary basis, awaiting the advent of any self-styled Moses to come to their rescue and take them out of America. By creating suspicion in the American mind as to the permanency or otherwise of the status of the American Jews, Ben-Gurion was helping every anti-Semite and strengthening their position.

But the astonishing thing was the attitude of the American Jews, who were caught between emotionalism and the exercise of their intelligence, and at long last rationalism prevailed over emotionalism. The leaders of American Jews were concerned with raising funds, so they brought a star attraction such as Ben-Gurion to aid the cause. In this pursuit, and in their emotionalism, the American Jewish leaders were able to overlook the insulting remarks of Ben-Gurion. However, it was the intelligence of the rank and file American Jews that finally prevailed over the emotionalism of their leaders. And so, despite the repeated demands of Mr. Ben-Gurion that American Jews should leave America in favor of Israel, not a single American Jew was willing to leave: It was a clear case of the rationalism of the American Jews overruling the emotionalism of their leaders.

On its part, and to its credit, the Action Committee on American-Arab Relations came out in defense of the American Jews. It sent telegrams to American Jewish leaders requesting them to renounce Ben-Gurion's continuous attacks upon American Jews and his threat to uproot the American Jewish community from America. Of course, the American Arabs were not only concerned with the welfare of their fellow citizens, the American Jews, but also were concerned with peace in the Middle East. The Action Committee on American-Arab Relations therefore repudiated Ben-Gurion, defending the right of the American Jews to stay permanently in America and in this stand, the American Arabs were joined by the rank and file American Jews. The American Council for Judaism also repudiated Ben-Gurion's attacks upon the American Jewish community.

17. According to the United Nations, the total Arab land which passed to Israeli hands is 16,324 square kilometers, of which 4,574 square kilometers are cultivable. The total area of Israel is 20,850 square kilometers. Thus 80% of the land under Israeli control belongs to the Palestinian Arab refugees (See United Nations Document A/1985). The Arabs in Israel own about 13% of the land, and the legally purchased and owned land of the Jews is about 6%.

The Arabs abandoned the entire cities of Jaffa, Acre, Lydda, Ramleh, Beit Shan, Migad Gad, plus 388 towns and villages, and large parts of 94 others; 10,000 shops, 120,000 dounam of orange groves, 40,000 dounam of vineyards, and at least 10,000 dounam of other orchards, and nearly 95% of the olive groves in the area. See Don Peretz, "Problems of Arab Refugee Compensation," MIDDLE EAST JOURNAL, Autumn 1954, pp. 403 ff.

Published By: New World Press
135 East 44th Street, New York, New York 10017